BILLY CALDWELL

1780–1841

Respecting the Revolutionary War when the Commander of the Forces solicited the Indians to join him, he promised that before he made peace with the Americans, there should be a boundary line drawn between the Indian Territory and the American ... the Indians who consider themselves greatly neglected by people who profess their friendship. It would be too tedious to mention every circumstance I was witness to for it would appear ridiculous to the world if it was known.

Billy Caldwell, Captain in the British Army, 1816

Native American Ten Commandments:

1. Treat the earth and all that dwell thereon with respect
2. Remain close to the Great Spirit
3. Show great respect for your fellow beings
4. Work together for the benefit of all Mankind
5. Give assistance and kindness wherever needed
6. Do what you know to be right
7. Look after the well-being of Mind and Body
8. Dedicate a share of your efforts to the greater good
9. Be truthful and honest at all times
10. Take full responsibility for your actions

BILLY CALDWELL

CHICAGO AND THE GREAT LAKES TRAIL

1780–1841

SUSAN L. KELSEY

AMERICA THROUGH TIME

America Through Time is an imprint of Sutton Publishing Inc
www.through-time.com
office@through-time.com

First published 2019
Reprinted 2025

ISBN 978-1-63499-186-5

Typeset in 10pt on 13pt Sabon
Printed and bound in England

Contents

All proceeds will be donated to Native American tribal initiatives

Timeline

1750 or 58:	William Caldwell (father) born at Caldwell Castle, Northern Ireland
1776, July 4:	Declaration of Independence adopted
1776:	William Caldwell in Niagara
1777:	William Caldwell appointed first captain of Butler's Rangers (British)
1778:	William Caldwell fought with Tecumseh in two famous battles
1779:	William Caldwell spent winter in Indian camp, Niagara and met Billy's mother
1780, March 17:	Billy Caldwell born outside of Fort Niagara (formerly in Canada)
1783:	William Caldwell married Susanne Baby, daughter of Jacques Duperon Baby
1784:	Billy (four years old) and mother, Sarah Rising Sun, moved to Six Nations Reserve
1786:	Father took Billy to Amherstburg, Ontario
1794:	Jay Treaty transferred Detroit to the United States.
1795:	Billy (fifteen years old) attended meeting with Blue Jacket and twenty-seven-year-old Tecumseh
1795, August 3:	Treaty of Greenville signed, ceding Chicago River property
1796:	Fort Malden established north of Caldwell property, town of Amherstburg grows
1797:	Billy (seventeen years old) began business relationship with John Forsyth and John Kinzie along the St. Joseph and Wabash Rivers.
1802:	William Caldwell donated land for new church
1803:	Fort Dearborn constructed. Billy appointed Fort Dearborn, clerk
1804:	Billy (twenty-four years old) met Alexander Robinson, married La Nanette, a Potawatomi who died after birth of first child,

	Alexander. She was niece of powerful Potawatomi Chief Mad Sturgeon
1804:	Louisiana Purchase finalized ceding 800,000 square miles to the western frontier
1804:	Billy Caldwell married La Nanette, daughter of White Sturgeon and niece of Chief Mad Sturgeon. La Nanette dies when son, Alexander, is born
1808–1812:	Billy Caldwell (twenty-eight years old) lived in Peoria
1811–1817:	War of 1812
1812, July 15:	Sold two smoked deerskins. No price stated. The traders sold Billy a pipe. Winter, returned to Amherstburg to enlist in service of British crown. Captain in Indian Department
1812, August 15:	Battle of Fort Dearborn
1812, August 16:	William Caldwell and his sons at Fort Detroit where Captain Hulls surrendered Detroit to the British
1813, January:	River Raisin, MI battle. Billy (thirty-three years old) was stabbed in neck, went back to Malden to recover
1813, October 4:	Battle of the Thames, Moravian Town. Tecumseh killed in battle
1814:	Billy Caldwell (thirty-four years old) second in command after his father
1815, August 25:	Received letter from Claus questioned him about responsibility, Billy Caldwell depressed, close to breakdown
1815, October 21:	Captain Billy Caldwell took charge and control over management of Indian Department
1816, August 16:	Letter from Billy Caldwell as captain of Indian Department
1816, September:	Billy Caldwell (thirty-six years old) is discharged. Tried to work in Amherstburg, but could not succeed
1818:	Billy Caldwell (thirty-eight years old) Headed to Ft. Dearborn, became fur trader, Inherited plot of land from father's death, but returned to U.S.
1818:	Illinois became the twenty-first state of the Union
1820:	Billy Caldwell (forty years old) moved to Chicago
1820, March 6:	Billy Caldwell was recommended to the governor as a suitable person to fill the office of Justice of the peace for Peoria. Wolcott was Indian agent
1822, February 22:	William Caldwell dies
1825:	Billy Caldwell (forty-five years old) elected Justice of the Peace
1825:	The Erie Canal opened, established new trade and migration routes
1826, August:	Judge in Peoria first election. This was the county seat
1827, April 27:	Billy Caldwell was recorded a buyer at estate, purchased fourteen ornamented waist belts, one Indian pipe, one piece blue calico, one man saddle
1828:	A frame house was built in Chicago for Billy Caldwell, on present-day SE corner of Chicago and State street
1828:	Billy Caldwell (forty-eight years old) had a daughter, Elizabeth (sixth child)

1829, July 27:	Council meetings appointed Billy as chief. Fabricated by Wolcott
1829, July 29:	Participated in treaty negotiation, Prairie du Chien
1829, July 29:	Negotiated land tracts for himself. Ratified January 2, 1830. Back to Chicago
1830:	Served as election judge
1830, June 9:	Beaubien received license for Sauganash Hotel
1830, August 2:	General election held in Peoria, Billy Caldwell one of thirty-two voting in election
1830, October 17–18:	Daughters, Helene and Susanne, baptized by Father Badin
1830, November 25:	I&M Canal; it was Billy who told James Bicklin, chief engineer of canal, to make a feeder of the calumet river
1832:	Against Blackhawk, Andrew Jackson reelected
1832, April:	Billy Caldwell wrote letter to Forsyth predicting the future, son, Alexander, died from alcoholism
1833:	Billy Caldwell (fifty-three years old) sold off his land, due to decline of fur trade
1833, September 10:	Treaty began at Fort Dearborn
1833, September 14:	Billy Caldwell questioned Governor Porter with united nations. All sides negotiated through Prairie du Chien
1833, September 16:	Billy Caldwell returned to fort, no answer
1833, September 26:	Treaty signed, agree to cede all lands between Lake Michigan and Mississippi, paying $1 million
1833, October 6:	Treaty is finalized, Billy Caldwell received a medal
1834, May 22:	Treaty ratified, Treaty of Chicago, Billy, $400 per year, plus $10,000
1834, November 18:	Married third wife, French/Potawatomi woman named Saqua LeGrand (born 1813). Led delegation of Indians and inspected their new reservation in Platte
1835:	Sometime in 1835, a delegation of Potawatomi Indians under Mr. Gordon visited Iowa, but stated it was too close to Sioux. Went south to junction of Kaw and Missouri River. Billy Caldwell's son, Charles, accompanied him on the trip
1835:	Billy Caldwell (fifty-five years old) and his band crossed the Mississippi River at Oquawka, Yellow Banks. Stopped on Skunk River in Iowa. Route through Fort Des Moines, Drew supplies from Ft. Leavenworth
1835, September 21:	Billy Caldwell left for west under guidance of Colonel J. B. F. Russell of U.S. Army. Chiefs Robinson, Caldwell, and LaFramboise proceeded to their place of rendezvous 12 miles from Chicago on the Des Plaines
1835, September 28:	Over 5,000 Native Americans left Chicago
1836:	Platte Purchase ratified
1836, September 17:	Treaty signed with Missouri Indians Platte purchase
1837:	Panic of 1837, lasted until 1840
1837, January 29:	Baptism of Susanne LaFramboise by Father Quickenborne. Caldwell was the godfather

1837, April:	Davis Hardin on Antelope Steamer, Council Bluffs, IA. Davis was appointed to instruct the band how to farm. Brought his family with him. He came from Leavenworth Kansas. $600 per year. Council Bluffs sub agency
1837, April:	Edwin James assigned blockhouse
1837, July 24:	Approximately 500 Potawatomi settled in Caldwell's Village, near the mission. Caldwell's family lived at Trader's Point (also his office). 2,000 Native Americans moved to Trader's Point
1837, July 28:	General Atkinson/Dr. Edwin James transported seventy-five to 100 women, children, and sick on steamer called *Kansas*
1837, August:	Billy and his tribe left for Council Bluffs, Iowa
1837, September 12:	Caldwell band requested a school and missionary
1837, November:	Blockhouse completed (Blockhouse removed in 1857)
1838:	Chief Bigfoot visits, then left for Des Moines River
1838, May 31:	Father Pierre-Jean De Smet and Father Felix Verreydt arrived in Council Bluffs
1838, July 20:	Added chapel and four cabins to blockhouse complex
1839, January 2:	Father De Smet, in a Catholic ceremony, married Billy Caldwell and Susanna Misnakwe—his fourth and final wife
1839, October:	De Smet left the Council Bluffs mission
1840, September 22:	Col. Steven W. Kearny and 165 dragoons left Fort Leavenworth, crossed over the Missouri toward the Potawatomi settlements and visited Council Bluffs, Iowa. Pottawatomi chiefs attending were Billy Caldwell, Joseph LaFramboise, Wam-go-see and Half Day. The dragoons left on October 7
1840, September 29:	U.S. Army camped on Mosquito Creek, supervised annuities distribution, and held council with the Indians
1840, October 31:	Commander Alexis Coiquillard met with the Potawatomi to discuss moving from Iowa to Kansas and the concept of "reuniting" the Potawatomi. "Sag-au-naw [?] "was principle spokesman and received approval of the plan from Burnett, Bourassa and others
1841:	Conversations continue about removal to Kansas
1841:	Billy (sixty-one years old) built mill at the expense of Caldwell's band.
1841, September 28:	Billy Caldwell (sixty-one years old) died of cholera at Traders Point. His body was carried to the Mission and buried on the bluff behind the mission. In 1890s, the body was moved to the "old Catholic" cemetery
1845–46:	Caldwell's wife died in Council Bluffs, Iowa
1846, July 22:	Treaty with Pottawatomie Nation.
1847:	Remaining Caldwell band moved to Kansas and Oklahoma Reservations, around 3,000 members
1859:	Chief Shabbona died, Morris, Illinois
1867, February 3:	Joseph LaFramboise died, Silver Lake, Kansas
1872:	Chief Alexander Robinson died, Chicago, Illinois
2015, May 11:	Billy Caldwell-Chief Sauganash historical marker dedication

Letter from William Whittaker, Research Director, Office of the State Archaeologist, University of Iowa

What to make of Billy Caldwell? He seemed to show up at every pivotal historic moment in the early nineteenth-century American frontier, running or being chased farther west with each episode, from upstate New York to the Missouri river bluffs of Iowa. Although a flesh-and-blood man, he was also the embodiment of white settlers' and government's ideas of what they thought Indians were or should be: the peacemaker alternative to Tecumseh, the compliant exemplar of what it was to not be Black Hawk. His name, his pedigree, his tribal affiliations are all in dispute. In white settlers' eyes, he was both a "civilized Indian," a cosmopolitan who could live in Chicago, and someone who could, through appearance, manners, and speech, navigate the world of the rich and powerful, but they also appointed him leader of the "savage Indians," in their racist eyes a homogenous grouping of unclean, feral, semi-humans. Some decried him as a traitor who fought against the U.S. and his seeming willingness to sell out his own people, but these same people were happy to use him as a tool to legitimize the dispossession of Indians from their land.

I would love to know what Caldwell thought of the capricious fate he endured, to read his unwritten autobiography. What agency did he possess over his life's events? He had influence and charisma, but no real power. His life was a series of forced retreats. The best he could do is try to negotiate and mitigate the horror of loss. From his actions and from what others recorded, he appeared to be deeply conflicted about his role; he seems to have reluctantly taken on leadership of the Potawatomi. Some historians, like O. J. Pruitt, claimed he cheated and stole from the Potawatomi, but this accusation was contradicted by Caldwell's choice. He could have abandoned them and returned to Chicago and lived his final years in comfort. Instead, he chose to remain with the Potawatomi during their exile to the forsaken frontier and he did his best to protect their interest and to negotiate their safety in a horrific time and place.

Susan Kelsey has taken on the seemingly impossible task of making sense of Caldwell's life; the available information about Caldwell is both overwhelming in its volume and frustrating in its contradictions and omissions. Black Hawk had Antoine Le Claire to help him put his life on paper, to translate the scope and tragedy and paradoxes of his life, and now Caldwell has Kelsey. Kelsey's dogged determination to find Caldwell under layers of myth led her on a voyage of discovery, both physically, as she followed his path across the continent, and intellectually, where she comes to terms with as complex a man as there ever was. We may never know Caldwell authentically, but Kelsey has clarified what we can and should know about this frontier icon, and reveals that, although the threads of history are transformed and obscured, they can lead us to make sense of the past and present of North America.

Letter from Dennis Downes, Author, sculptor, founder of the Great Lakes Trail Marker Tree Society

For centuries, Native Americans used many different means to mark the boundaries between their tribal territories and hunting grounds, as well as to mark their trails and convey important messages. Some of these markers were upright standing stones; others were pictographs or petroglyphs; symbols were painted or carved on to trees, large earthen mounds, and even intentionally shaped trees or Trail Marker Trees were utilized. Native American Trail Marker Trees are culturally modified trees that were part of an extensive land and water navigation system that was in place long before the first European settlers arrived in North America. These trees had distinctive shapes and characteristics that would differentiate them from other trees that may have had natural deformities or anomalies. By utilizing trees, the Indians had a flexible sapling that was easy to shape while young, which would develop into a solid marker that would last for centuries.

Billy Caldwell and his compatriots would have seen and utilized these trail markers around the Great Lakes, along the shoreline, by interior rivers, and throughout Indian Country. The French, Spanish, and British explorers realized early on that this "secret" navigation system was dependable and extensive. Many tribes were now working in unfamiliar areas either by being pushed out of their homeland or themselves working in the fur trade, again resulting in the need for a system of marking routes in unfamiliar territory.

Many of our famous first residents of the Chicagoland area were either Native American, part Native American, or married into Native American tribes: Jean Baptiste Pointe Du Sable, Gurdon Saltonstall Hubbard, Antoine Ouilmette, Billy Caldwell, and Alexander Robinson. Their occupation in the fur trade would have put them in constant contact with the ancient trail marker trees that were already in the area, using them as landmarks of their own and shaping saplings to mark new trails and portage routes for faster delivery of furs.

One of the earliest documented examples of a standing stone marker in North America, was recorded by Conrad Weiser in 1748 near modern-day Huntingdon,

Pennsylvania. Weiser was a pioneer, interpreter, judge, and worked for the provincial government. In his teens, Weiser lived among the Mohawk tribe to learn their language and practices. This standing stone stood along the banks of the Juniata River in Pennsylvania; it was documented to be at least 14 feet tall, 6 inches in width, and 6 inches in depth. The stone had ancient writings and symbols carved into it to convey information. It was referred to by numerous early explorers and settlers until it was removed in 1754. Around that time, oral orders were given by the British to remove anything that indicated higher intelligence and communication skills possessed by the native inhabitants of the land. This practice does explain the disappearance of other standing stones that were mentioned in numerous states in the 1700s and 1800s. Although, it is said that the Huntingdon standing stone was removed by the Oneida. A memorial replica of this stone was erected on September 8, 1896, in Huntingdon, Pennsylvania, that is still standing today.

Today, Native Americans tribes and nations are working with the Great Lakes Trail Marker Tree Society to identify, protect, honor, and preserve these heritage trees. Less than a few hundred are left in the United States and finding one is a moment to treasure and admire.

Introduction

Treat the earth well: it was not given to you by your parents, it was loaned to you by your children. We do not inherit the Earth from our Ancestors, we borrow it from our Children.

Tribe Unknown

Billy Caldwell, a Métis born March 17, 1780 outside of Fort Niagara, New York (then Canada), to Rising Sun, Mohawk Nation, and William Caldwell, an Irish captain in the British army. Caldwell was an influential leader during the dawn of America and one whose story transcends history with a man fighting for his family, a way of life, and, ultimately, a home for his tribe. He found himself at the crossroads of a new America, caught between two worlds—a quickly descending minority world of Native Americans and the growing white settlement spreading west across the country. He navigated the two worlds by creating commerce in the Great Lakes region, following opportunities across the country, and building a community for his family and friends.

Situated in a unique position in 1833, Caldwell was named chief for the three Chicago tribes—Ottawa, Ojibwa, and Potawatomi (also spelled Pottawattomi)—and negotiated one of the largest land trades in American history. This treaty represented over 5 million acres, allowing white settlement to move into the Midwest and Lake Michigan and removing thousands of Native Americans to Indian Territory west of the Missouri River.

No known picture exists today of the late Billy Caldwell, also called Sauganash (meaning English speaking). While he was a prominent figure during the beginning of Chicago, not much was known about his life before arriving in Chicago and what happened to him after he left Chicago in 1837. This book research stretched across two countries, eleven states, and numerous visits to tribal nations, historic museums, libraries, and personal interviews to capture the facts of Billy Caldwell's life starting in 1780 outside of Fort Niagara, moving as he did and ending in Council Bluffs, Iowa, on

September 27, 1841. Since the history and geography over Billy Caldwell's lifetime is so expansive, this book focuses on historic events and locations that relate to the Billy Caldwell story. Over the centuries, researchers have asked questions about who Billy Caldwell was as a person, why did he migrate from the eastern Great Lakes, through New York, Canada, Michigan, Indiana, Illinois, Wisconsin, and Iowa? Why did he leave Chicago when his compatriots stayed in Illinois? What caused his move from Platte County, Missouri, to Iowa? Billy Caldwell has fascinated researchers and readers for more than 250 years. Based on existing research by noted authors such as James A. Clifton, R. David Edmonds, Charles Babbitt, O. J. Pruitt, and Ann Durkin Keating, Caldwell's life was pieced together with interesting facts about his early life, how he provided for his family, and, in the end, how he created community with his tribe in Iowa and led an independent life as Métis on the new frontier.

Diversity Defined

Over the years, race and ethnic definitions have changed according to politics, geography, wars, and compassion. The term "Indian" was first used mid-fifteenth century. Following the civil rights movement in America, many ethnicities were changed to include the word "American." The term, "Native American" was created in the twentieth century and is most commonly used today in America. There is a movement by tribal nations to a preferred term, "Indigenous Nations," and, concurrently, a replacement of Columbus Day, the second Monday in October, to Indigenous Peoples' Day. In Canada, tribal nations are called "First Nations." Adding to the fluid geopolitical lines between Canada and the United States is the history of Six Nations. Six Nations is a confluence of six tribes, originally from the present-day U.S. side of the border, migrating up to Canada during the War of 1812. The six nations include Mohawk, Seneca, Oneida, Onondaga, Cayuga, and the Tuscarora, and now reside in Canada. For the purposes of this book, the term Native American is used to respect the current federally recognized nations and all indigenous people in the United States. Reference to "Indian" is used in historical context and from documented resources. Lastly, Native Americans share that it is proper to refer to Caldwell as the "late Billy Caldwell" out of respect for his spirit.

1

Ice, Mastodons, and Mammals

When your time comes to die, be not like those whose hearts are filled with fear of death, so that when their time comes, they weep and pray for a little more time to live their lives over again in a different way. Sing your death song and die like a hero going home.

Tecumseh

The Great Lakes, formed by ice glaciers thousands of years ago, create the largest freshwater source in the world. Bordered by the United States and Canada, the Great Lakes include the megalopolis regions of Illinois, Indiana, Michigan, Minnesota, New York, Ohio, Pennsylvania, and Wisconsin, as well as the Canadian province of Ontario.

The Great Lakes are one of the largest economic units in the world with over $6 trillion of U.S. G.D.P. and has always been the center of trade and commerce. The Great Lakes geographic region is defined by Montreal on the east, the American–Canadian Lake of the Woods on the west, and the city of St. Louis at the crossroads of the Ohio and Mississippi River on the south. With 87 percent of North America's freshwater, the book explores the area's geological formation and its role in human history; its diverse plant, bird, and animal species; and its significant physical, climatic, and environmental features. The Great Lakes are a series of interconnected freshwater lakes in the United States and Canada. They connect to the Atlantic through the St. Lawrence River.

Following the retreat of the ice glaciers, the Great Lakes served as a watering hole for historic mastodons, extinct mammals that looked like present-day elephants. The mastodons blazed trails around the Great Lakes, followed by more contemporary mammals and eventually humans.

The scientific name for the specific glacier that covered the Midwest and Great Lakes is the Laurentide Ice Sheet—commonly known as the Wisconsin Glacier. Over the course of millions of years, the retreat and advance of the glacier created what we know today

Laurentide Glacier, also known as the Wisconsin Glacier. The Wisconsin Glacier retreated around 11,000 years ago, leaving the five Great Lakes. (*Image courtesy of the Illinois State Geological Survey, Prairie Research Institute, Quaternary Glaciations in Illinois, isgs.illinois.edu/outreach/geology-resources/quaternary-glaciations-illinois*)

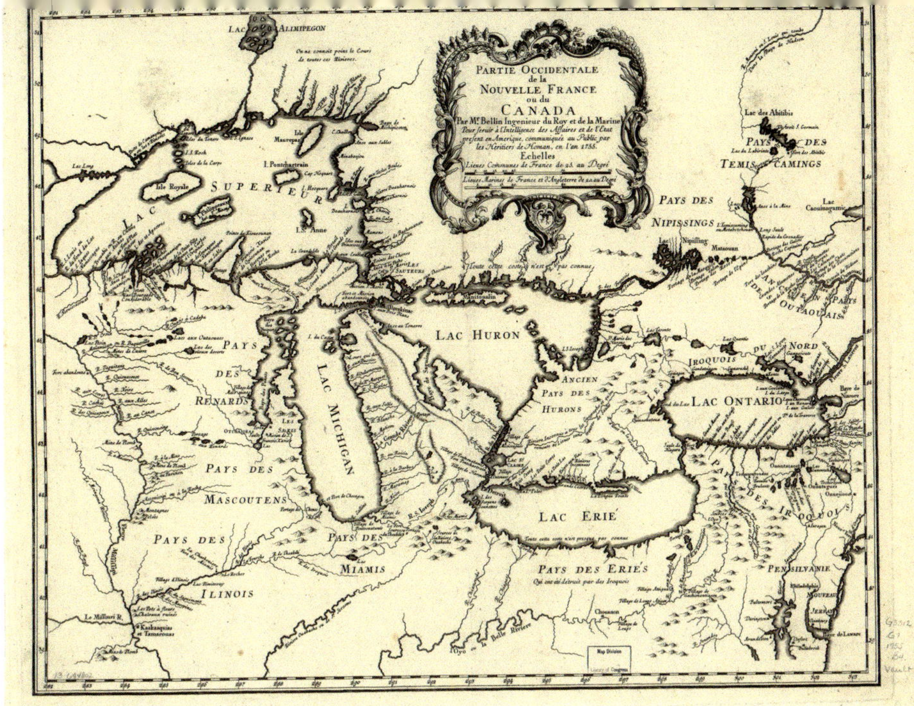

Above: Partie occidentale de la Nouvelle France ou Canada. A 1755 map created by French cartographer Jacques-Nicolas Bellin (1703 to March 21, 1772). The map, created at the beginning of the French-Indian War, illustrates the vast Indian villages and their relationship with the French fur traders and explorers. (*Image reproduced from Susan L. Kelsey private collection, also located at U.S. Library of Congress, Bellin, Jacques Nicolas. Partie occidentale de la Nouvelle France ou Canada. [Paris?, 1755] Map. www.loc.gov/item/73695755*)

Below: Niagara River and rapids on the American side of the falls around 1900. (*Image courtesy of the Library of Congress, Detroit Publishing Co., Publisher. American Rapids, www.loc.gov/item/2016794557*)

about the Great Lakes and the geography in the Midwest. According to the Illinois State Geological Survey at the Prairie Research Institute, the glaciers would advance and retreat, bringing with them rock and ice, scraping the earth for hundreds of miles and creating the rich soil, vast landscape, and lake/river system we have today in the Great Lakes region.

An important and strategic result of the Wisconsin Glacier was the creation of the Niagara River. The Niagara River is located at the northeast end of Lake Erie and flows north to Lake Ontario, about 35 miles in length. According to the National Park Service, Department of the Interior: "Historically, the Niagara River served as the gateway to the west with Native Americans and early European explorers portaging around Niagara Falls to travel to the interior of the North America. It was a core part of the extensive trade route that brought fur pelts from America's interior to Europe via the Great Lakes and the St. Lawrence River." The Niagara Falls is a natural phenomenon releasing energy and power, and contains its own tides, waterspouts, fogs and thunderstorms, mirages, and even icebergs. These natural highways are the basis for today's highways and interstates, having covered much of the original trails left thousands of years ago.

Native Americans utilized the Niagara River, Great Lakes, and other waterways as a source of commerce, community, and transportation. Water routes, streams, and rivers were at the crossroads of trade and a communications network. Waterways were the main thoroughfare along with portages, forts, and trading posts.

Dennis Downes, author of *Native American Trail Marker Trees: Marking Paths through the Wilderness* (2011), states: "Before paved roads, street signs, railroads, and road maps, the Native Americans created a navigational system of their own to aid them in their travels."

According to Dennis, the Trail Marker Trees were bent into a horizontal shape with a distinguishing appearance so the trail could easily be marked. The horizontal line was not a natural shape, perhaps similar to a deer, so the eye could easily discern the marker on the trail. These Trail Marker Trees indicated "exits" off the trail as well as fresh spring water locations. There are many sizes and shapes of Trail Marker Trees, many still preserved today throughout the United States.

Trails around the Great Lakes have been used for hundreds of years. As the glacier retreated around 11,000–14,000 years ago, humans began to populate the region and, into the early 1600s, it was a new frontier for Europeans and explorers. Prior to the birth of Billy Caldwell, during the late 1600s, the French and the British fought four wars for control of the Indigenous Nations and North America. The stakes were high, and the wars were fierce. Shifting alliances between the Native Americans and the three countries created a confusing roadmap. By the end of the French and Indian War (the Seven Years' War), the British had won control over the former French territory in the Midwest. Billy's father, William Caldwell, was a captain in the British Army and was part of this activity. What the French already knew, the British had learned how important it was to create alliances with the Native American population during this time.

At the center of the battles was a race for resources in the new America. An important influence happening concurrently, was the emergence of a new company called the Hudson Bay Company. Indigenous people, already familiar with the Great Lakes trails and waterways, were an important partner to Europeans to navigate the new world.

Above left: This trail marker tree was located in Lake Forest, Illinois, providing directional access between Lake Michigan and the Des Plaines River. Indian Trail Marker Trees were used for navigation, like modern-day highway systems. (*Image courtesy of Dennis Downes*)

Above right: This Traverse City, Michigan, Trail Marker Tree has been recognized and protected by its community and local Native American Tribes for over a century. The Grand Traverse County Parks and Recreation Department organized an event to honor the Trail Marker Tree as well as the Grand Traverse Band of Ottawa and Chippewa Indians who funded the granite engraved bolder and the new protective fence surrounding the tree. (*Image courtesy of Dennis Downes*)

Below: A 1785 map of Hudson Bay Company (H.B.C.) with detailed North American waterways, rivers, lakes, and trails. At one time, the H.B.C. covered more that 40 percent of Canada from the Artic to the Great Lakes. (*Image courtesy of Library of Congress. Kohl, J. G, and Peter Pond. Hudson's Bay's country. [1850] Map. www.loc.gov/item/2002622133*)

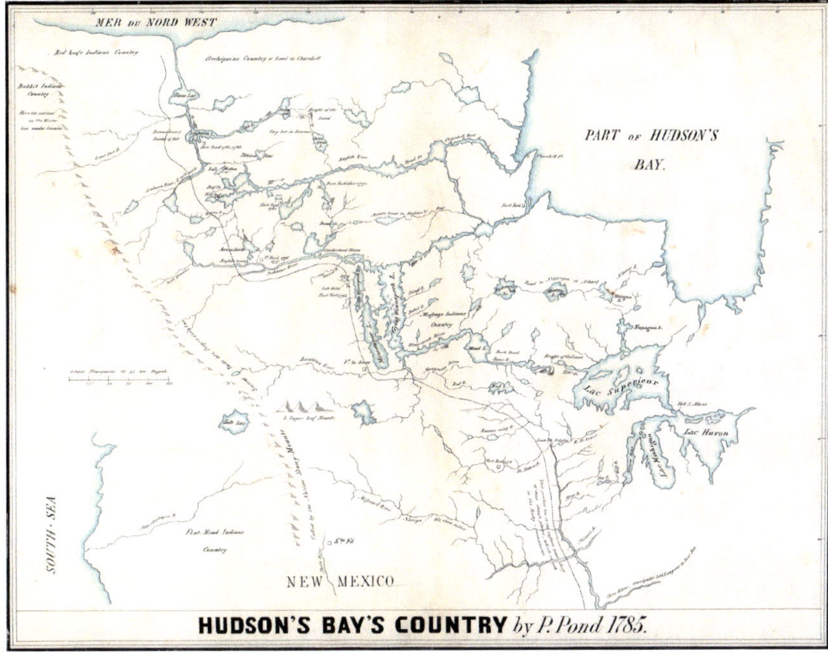

The Hudson Bay Company was founded in 1670 by the Governor and Company of Adventurers of England to exploit the fur trade in the new America. The company is still the oldest incorporated joint-stock merchandising company in the English-speaking world. King Charles II of England grated a royal charter to the business that became the Hudson Bay Company. The Hudson Bay Company learned to integrate themselves with the Indigenous Nations population where they learned more about the geography of the land and how to trade with existing resources.

The Hudson Bay point blanket was traded by the company in North America during the 1700s and 1800s with First Nations in exchange for beaver pelts. The wool blankets had four stripes, green, red, yellow, and indigo on a white background, produced with strong dyes. Today, this trademark blanket is still sold.

Intermarriage between fur traders and natives ensured communications leading to strategic commerce relationships. Various languages, but common dialects, were spoken throughout the Great Lakes region, allowing extensive travel throughout the area. The vast water region forms a distinctive historical, economic, and cultural identity.

This identity defined the life of Billy Caldwell. Over his lifetime, his journey around the Great Lakes was complexly threaded through his livelihoods, his journey across the regions, and, ultimately, to his removal from the area with the Indian Removal Act of the 1830s. The geography and waterways left by the glaciers provided transportation, a lifestyle, food, nourishment, and commerce. Each of these elements shaped the life of Billy Caldwell and impacted his thoughts on land, family, commerce, alliances, loyalty, and, ultimately, finding a final home for his people.

These experiences set into context what we know today about the decision Caldwell made when he negotiated the Treaty of Chicago (1833), which ceded over 5 million acres to the new America for westward expansion. It helps the reader to understand why Caldwell migrated west throughout his life, following the ancient glacial trails and developing a fur-trading livelihood. It helps to understand how Caldwell made a life-changing and final decision to move west with his people instead of remaining in Chicago. Lastly, the land and the geography help the reader to understand how Caldwell understood the importance of the land by creating commerce at the origination point of the soon-to-be new frontier Oregon Trail.

It is on the Niagara River that the Billy Caldwell story began, outside of Fort Niagara, located in present-day New York. Prior to the birth of Caldwell in 1780, a young America was emerging. The region was a bustling commerce of fur trading, multiple nations, and personalities.

It was during this time that a young Billy Caldwell was born to a Mohawk woman and a father who was a captain in the British Army. Billy was born on the shores of Lake Ontario and the Niagara River at a time of turbulence for the region and changing geopolitical ties and boundary lines. Caldwell was born on British soil, just outside of Fort Niagara, in present-day New York. His father was of Irish descent, having emigrated into the country from Ireland around 1773. His mother was Mohawk, with her clan having emigrated from the present-day upstate New York region as part of the migration of Native Americans to join forces with the British. The fluidity of the political boundaries, alliances, and resources continued throughout the Great Lakes region for two centuries.

H.B.C. point blankets (and jackets) were made of wool material varying in cut, style, and decoration. Colors included a green stripe, red stripe, yellow stripe, and indigo stripe on a white background. Points or short black lines were woven into the edge of the blanket to allow traders to quickly see the size of the blanket when it was folded. (*Image courtesy of Susan L. Kelsey*)

North American Indian village watercolor artwork. (*Image courtesy of the Susan L. Kelsey private collection, artist unknown*)

Fort Niagara, New York. Built over 300 years ago on the edge of Lake Ontario and the Niagara River, Fort Niagara controlled access to the Great Lakes and the westward route through a new nation. (*Image courtesy of Susan L. Kelsey*)

A wonderful 1771 map showing the confluence of Six Nations (Native Indian tribes) and their relationship to the eastern colonies. Note the Six Nations located in the present-day state of New York and Finger Lake region. Later, Six Nations moved to Canada where today they exist on over 46,000 acres, only 5 percent of the original 950,000, from the 1784 Haldimand Treaty. This information is from pp. 432–433 of *A History of the Schenectady Patent in the Dutch and English Times* by Jonathan Pearson, (Albany, NY: J. Munsell's Sons, Printers, 1883). (*Image courtesy of the Schenectady Collection of the Schenectady County Public Library at Schdy R 974.744 P36*)

The first Indigenous population in the area were the Iroquoian Nation (Seneca's, Cayuga's, Onondagas, Oneidas, and the Mohawk) and the Algonquin Nation (the Ottawa's, the Ojibwas, and the Potawatomi).

As Caldwell began his life, he moved across these lines and, throughout his life, continued to blend and lead these shifting alliances and paths into a career that spanned across all the Great Lakes and trail systems.

Overall, the disruption of Indigenous People's lives over the century has compounded the confusion of facts, geography, and history. Helen Hornbeck Tanner states it best in her book, *Atlas of the Great Lakes Indian History*:

> ... factors in the complex picture of this part of North America have been territorial conquest by inter-tribal warfare; refugee movements; epidemics; French-English trade rivalry; inter-tribal alliances; encroachment by settlers; Indian treaties ceding land to state and national governments with imperfectly administered arrangements for reservations, removal, and land allotments.

All these factors were considered when researching, evaluating, and understanding history, particularly over the lifespan of Billy Caldwell.

By the eighteenth century, waves of Native Americans were displaced from the east and migrated to the Great Lakes region. By the early nineteenth century, the Midwest native population had either negotiated for land, existing reservations by today's standards, or had moved west during the Indian Removal Act. There was a race for resources such as land, transportation, waterways, and commerce. The tidal wave of new settlers moving to the frontier land was unstoppable.

North American Native American village watercolor painting. (*Image courtesy of the Susan L. Kelsey private collection, artist unknown*)

American Fur Company buildings at Fond du Lac, head of Lake Superior. From McKenny, *Tour to the Lakes*. (*Image courtesy of the Library of Congress, American Fur Cos. buildings. Fond du Lac back view. Fond Du Lac Wisconsin, 1827. Photograph. www.loc.gov/item/2007683613/*)

While the indigenous people had worked well with the French for hundreds of years, the quick advance of the Americans and white settlers left indigenous populations in the minority. In a relatively short time, native populations around the Eastern Seaboard were displaced from their native land, moved west, and encroached upon other tribes indigenous to the area. Within a period of 200 years, the Native American home landscape was changed forever.

2

1780: The Shifting Landscape

Remember that your children are not your own, but are lent to you by the Creator.

Mohawk

Caldwell's story began outside the walls of the Old Fort Niagara at the junction of Lake Ontario and the Niagara River. The fort is located about 15 miles north of Niagara Falls on the U.S. border. Billy Caldwell was born outside of Fort Niagara, located on the south side of Lake Ontario, east of the Niagara River. The fort was a strategic location for countries expanding into the New World because it controlled the navigable waters between the Great Lakes and access to the fur trade. Some 300 years ago, indigenous people used the location for hunting and fishing. Built by the French in 1721, the fort was, and still is, a large castle on the edge of the Niagara River. For the next 300 years, the fort was a shifting landscape held by the French, British, and Americans. Billy Caldwell's mother, Mohawk Rising Sun from the New York Mohawk Valley, lived outside the fort walls. Following the American Revolution in 1776, many of the Mohawk members in the New York valley aligned with the British and moved up north to Fort Niagara for protection, food, and supplies.

According to the Old Fort Niagara Association (est. 1927), "during the colonial wars in North America, a fort at the mouth of the Niagara River was vital, for it controlled access to the Great Lakes and the westward route to the heartland of the continent." Fort Niagara served as the Loyalist base in New York during the American Revolutionary War for Butler's Rangers. The glaciers left a remarkable natural and strategic land formation between Lake Ontario and Lake Erie, with the Niagara River connecting the two.

During the American Revolution, Fort Niagara's job was to protect the portage for military and commercial use and to continue the fur trading on the Great Lakes.

Historic Fort Niagara located on Lake Ontario and Niagara River. Three flags are flown daily representing the three nations that held Fort Niagara: France, Britain, and the United States. (*Image courtesy of Susan L. Kelsey*)

Map located at Six Nations Museum detailing connections between Lake Ontario and Lake Erie. (*Image by Susan L. Kelsey courtesy of Six Nations Museum*)

The New York Finger Lakes, remnants of the last glacier, include Lake Ontario, eleven lakes, rolling hills, 1,063 waterfalls, 100 miles of the Erie Canal, and 400 historic sites. Native American legend states a Great Spirit blessed the land with his hands leaving the shape of his fingers behind. Six Nations originated in the Finger Lakes region and moved to the Canada reserve at the turn of the eighteenth century. (*Image by Susan L. Kelsey*)

The Niagara River separates Erie Lake and Ontario Lake and was controlled by the powerful Six Nations. The fort door featured has five Indian Nations carved in the shield above the door. The French carved the entrance of the fort to honor five tribes, not knowing a sixth tribe, the Tuscarora, was coming. Because of slow communication during those days, eventually the Tuscarora Indians arrived at Fort Niagara and it was renamed Six Nations.

According to Tanner, it was the 1783 Treaty of Paris that really revealed the American intention of wanting Indian land west of the Ohio River. Caldwell, three years old at the time, would have had a unique perspective on this early in his life and throughout his career along the Great Lakes. It was during this treaty that the British relinquished a large part of the region and agreed to a boundary line between the United States and Canada, which follows today's existing international border.

Billy Caldwell's father, William, was born around 1750 in Northern Ireland and arrived in North America around 1773 where he fought in the American Revolution for Butler's Rangers. Here, Caldwell, Sr., met Billy's mother, Rising Sun. Soon after, Billy was born—on St. Patrick's Day, 1780. Caldwell, Sr., left Rising Sun and Billy and moved south to the east side of the Detroit River where he married French-Canadian Suzanne Baby. They had five sons and three daughters (Mary, William, James, Susanna, Thomas, William Francis, John, Therese, and Elizabeth).

Billy Caldwell was a Métis (MAY-tee), a person of mixed ancestry, usually Native American and European. Many of the families that associated with Billy throughout his lifetime were of French Métis descent. During the fur-trading period, Métis people were important to the Great Lakes region and facilitated trade, communication, and

Entrance to Fort Niagara with seal above doorway. The Gate of Five Nations (from 1756–1805) insignia includes: Mohawk, Onondaga, Seneca, Oneida, and Cayuga. (*Image by Susan L. Kelsey*)

diplomacy between the Natives and Europeans. Most Métis, like Billy, spoke French (a native language) and usually several dialects of regional native languages. Biracial people in the Great Lakes, Chicago, and Iowa areas included Billy Caldwell, Alexander Robinson, and members of the Beaubien, Ouilmette, Chevalier, Bourassa, Mirandeau, and LaFramboise families.

A fierce and ruthless soldier, Caldwell, Sr., fought in numerous battles at Sandusky River (Ohio) and Kentucky. At the end of the war, Caldwell and Indian Agent Matthew Elliott began developing large parcels of land around Fort Malden and the newly emerging town of Amherstburg. Over time, he acquired over 2,000 acres of land, was a prominent figure in Amherstburg, a leader in the British movement, and died and was buried in his hometown.

Meanwhile, while Billy Caldwell was growing up at the camp outside of Fort Niagara, an influential leader by the name of Joseph "Thayendanegea" Brant (1742–1807) led Mohawk and other First Nations. He built community within the nations and would have been a strong influence in the young Billy Caldwell's life. A significant British officer and Mohawk chief, Brant was an important leader in the American Revolution

Image of Chief Thayendanegea located at the St. Joseph Area Historical Society Museum. St. Joseph, Missouri. (*Image by Susan L. Kelsey courtesy of the St. Joseph Area Historical Society Museum*)

and as a spokesperson for the Six Nations. Brant's grandfather, Sagayeathquapiethtow, went to England in 1710 to visit Queen Anne. He was one of "The Four Indian Kings" and his portrait hangs in museums around the world. Joseph Brant dedicated his life to fighting for the rights of the Six Nations.

Rising Sun's Mohawk tribe would have been one of the six nations that camped outside of the fort during that time. Displaced from the New York valley, her tribe was dependent on the British for food and supplies.

The winter of 1779–80, when Billy was born, was one of the most severe on record. The winter was long and hard with more than 8 feet of snow, and many did not survive. Billy would have been less than a year old through that hard winter. Snow and intense cold covered the ground all winter. In the spring, bodies of horses and cattle were found in the woods where they had perished from exposure and starvation. The winter of 1785–86 was also one of extreme cold and deep snow. As late as March 1, 1786, the snow was 4 feet deep in places where it had not been disturbed. In Lake St. Clair, the ice was 3 feet thick a mile from the shore and did not disappear until May.

In May 1784, Brant relocated many of the Fort Niagara natives to "Brant's Settlement" outside of Fort Niagara in compensation for their losses in the war. Billy and his mother followed Brant to these locations. Billy's father fought with Brant, particularly in violent wars around the early 1780s. After his retirement, Brant was "chief of chiefs," meaning he was the highest chief of all Six Nations.

The Joseph Brant Monument was erected by the city of Brantford, Ontario, in recognition of the loyalist Mohawk leader, Joseph Brant, who fought on the side of the British during the Revolutionary War. Following the war, in 1784, Joseph Brant

Outside the walls of Fort Niagara, this would have been the location of where Mohawk Nation would have camped in 1780. (*Image by Susan L. Kelsey*)

Inside Fort Niagara, looking west over the Niagara River. This would have been a busy access point to the fort. (*Image by Susan L. Kelsey*)

Joseph Brant, Mohawk leader.
(*Image by Susan L. Kelsey*)

received a land grant from Sir Frederick Haldimand as restitution for their losses in the war. This is called the Six Nations Reserve, located just outside of Brantford. The Joseph "Thayendanegea" Brant Monument is in Victorian Square in Brantford, Ontario. Percy Wood, a famous British sculptor, won the international design competition. After two visits to Canada to make sketches of the Six Nations people, he sculpted this wonderful memorial. This memorial is one of the first pieces of statuary of its kind in North America. The monument is made of bronze and granite. The bronze used for this monument came from cannons, donated by the British Government, which had been used at Waterloo (1815) and in the Crimean War (1853–1856). Famous Six Nations poetess Pauline Johnson wrote a poem for the occasion.

According to the Joseph Brant Museum, Brant led the Mohawks and other tribes to Mohawk Village, 80 miles west of Fort Niagara, on the Grand River. According to historical markers, allies of the British during the American War of Independence, the Six Nations Iroquois, received extensive lands along the Grand River in 1784. Mohawks, led by Joseph Brant, established a village of some 400 inhabitants by 1788. The community was situated at an important crossing point on the river (Brant's Ford) and prospered as a resting place for travellers on the Detroit Trail that linked the Niagara and Detroit Rivers. Later, in 1841, the Canadian Government moved the Grand River Iroquois and Mohawk tribes to a second location on their land south of the river. Only the Mohawk Chapel remains on the original land.

In Mohawk Village, a chapel was built in 1785 called Her Majesty's Royal Chapel of the Mohawks. It is located high on a bluff overlooking the Grand River.

Above: Former site of Mohawk Village located on the eastern edge of the Grand River. (*Image by Susan L. Kelsey courtesy of Six Nations on the Grand River*)

Below: Mohawk Church, the only structure left from Mohawk Village, located on the Six Nations Reserve. (*Image by Susan L. Kelsey courtesy of Six Nations on the Grand River*)

The chapel is the oldest-surviving church in Ontario and is one of the two Royal Chapels in north America. Five Nations from the Mohawk Valley in New York pledged their allegiance to the crown and asked for a Chapel.

Queen Anne presented the chapel with a bible, silver communion service, and prayer books. The chapel was completed in 1785. Billy and his mother attended this chapel.

The chapel is also the location of Joseph Brant's tomb—in an iron-fenced section just south of the chapel. Brant died in 1807 at his home in Burlington, Ontario. He was an Iroquois and part of the alliance of Native Americans including the Mohawk (Caldwell's mother) at the beginning of the American War for Independence.

Born in 1742 near Akron, Ohio, he was educated in English language and fought for the British as a warrior and strategist. According to the Burlington Museum Foundation, Brant travelled to London to visit King George III to ensure his people would receive the promised lands.

The Mohawk Chapel is located on the Six Nations of the Grand River, Canada. It was created from the Haldimand Treaty of 1784. The treaty provided for over 950,000 acres to Six Nations for the loss of their settlements in New York Hudson Valley after the 1776 war. Today, 46,500 acres remain, with more than 13,000 people living at Six Nations.

Around 1787, Billy's father took him from his mother at Six Nations. Billy would have been around seven or eight years old. His father was newly married to Suzanne Baby, a French-Canadian woman from a prominent family. During Billy's formative teenage years, he was brought up in a white world, Jesuit-schooled, and learned English and French—which served him greatly as he became a leader in Chicago. According to Clifton, Billy's father placed little value on his relationship with his son and Billy's mother. Soon after Billy was born, his father left for war in Detroit. He busied himself with land speculations and trading enterprises and started development of his personal estate in Amherstburg, which would later play an integral role in Billy's lifetime.

By the time Billy was twenty years old, he had experienced life as an outsider, as an Indigenous person, a British ally, an insider as a white, Jesuit-schooled student, a Métis in Canada and Detroit, and a son of a British Army captain. Clifton, whose studies focused on the various influences in the young Caldwell's life, created a composite of possible perspectives Billy may have had in his life. As Caldwell moved through his twenties, he began to align himself with business people, friends, and leaders that guided him, used him, and befriended him for the next few decades.

According to the H.M. Royal Chapel of the Mohawks website, the Mohawks who remained loyal to the British Crown would leave their homeland and relocate to Upper Canada. Discover the roles, relationships, and values the Mohawks would live in the late 1700s to the early 1800s. Her Majesty's Royal Chapel of the Mohawks is the last remaining building of the Mohawk Village built in 1785. (*Image by Susan L. Kelsey courtesy of Six Nations on the Grand River*)

Her Majesty's Royal Chapel of the Mohawks was the first Protestant Church in Upper Canada, and is now the oldest surviving church in Ontario. (*Image by Susan L. Kelsey courtesy of Six Nations on the Grand River*)

Above: Tomb of Captain Joseph Brant, located at Mohawk Chapel. Joseph Brant, known as Thayendanegea, was a warrior who led his followers across Lake Ontario. In 1784, after the Haldimand Proclamation was issued, Joseph Brant led a group of Six Nations people to what is now Brantford. In 1785, the Mohawk Chapel was built. According to JosephBrant.com website, Brant fought to win the hearts of Indian people and put loyalty to the Six Nations before loyalty to the British. Although Brant did not manage to unite Native Americans into permanent union, he paved the way for future Indian Chiefs, most notably Shawnee leader Tecumseh who was instrumental in the formation of the great tribal confederacy that declared open war against Americans in 1810s. (*Image by Susan L. Kelsey courtesy of Six Nations on the Grand River*)

Below: Jane Wells is pleading for her life, and a man attempts to protect her from an Indian who is about to kill her. The house behind them is being burned by Loyalists and Indians led by Major Walter Butler and Mohawk Chief Joseph Brant, Cherry Valley, New York. From the original picture by A. Chappel; Thomas Phillibrown, engraver. Cherry Valley New York, *c.* 1856. N.Y.: Martin, Johnson & Co. publishers. (*Image courtesy of the Library of Congress. www.loc.gov/item/94506098*)

Left: Six Nations Reserve located on the Grand River near Ontario, Canada. Established during the American Revolution, it is home to approximately 27,000 members on 46,000 acres. This represents approximately 5 percent of the original 950,000 acres of land granted to the Six Nations by the 1784 Haldimand Treaty. (*Image by Susan L. Kelsey courtesy of Six Nations on the Grand River*)

Below: Six Nations map representing community, businesses and tribal interests. Visitors are welcomed to the reserve. The Six Nations website states there are over 300 businesses on the reserve. (*Image by Susan L. Kelsey courtesy of Six Nations on the Grand River*)

3

1790: Battling for Resources

Seek wisdom, not knowledge. Knowledge is of the past, Wisdom is of the future.

Lumbee

Soon after the turn of the nineteenth century, the pace quickened and the battle for resources accelerated. The westward push for resources along the Great Lakes was moving quickly and parties were fighting for land and water, all the while expanding west.

Early in Caldwell's life, his father, William Caldwell (1750–1822), began developing tracts of land on the east side (now Canadian side) of the Detroit River, later to be named Amherstburg, Ontario. The Caldwell family received one of the largest tracts of land on the frontier and assembled about 2,000 acres in the new community.

In 1777, Butler's Rangers were formed. William Caldwell was commissioned a captain and led several well-documented attacks during the American Revolution. The 1794 Treaty of Canandaigua created a lasting peace and friendship between the Six Nations and the United States. It was signed November 11, 1794, and ratified January 21, 1795. Over the last 200 years, this important treaty has been upheld in courts and land claims, and today is still cited in law cases.

The 1794 Treaty of Greenville Peace Medals were awarded and, according to researchers, Billy Caldwell received a medal like the one shown in the photo.

Built in 1795, Fort Malden was a strategic military defense post for Britain. Located across the Detroit River from present-day Detroit, historic Fort Malden sits on the site of the former Fort Amherstburg. During the times, the forts switched ownership and control between the British and Americans several times.

Further west, at Lake Michigan, during the Treaty of Greenville, 1795, the Potawatomi sold the tract of land around the Chicago River leading into Lake Michigan. This included the 1803 building of a new Fort Dearborn at the mouth of the Chicago

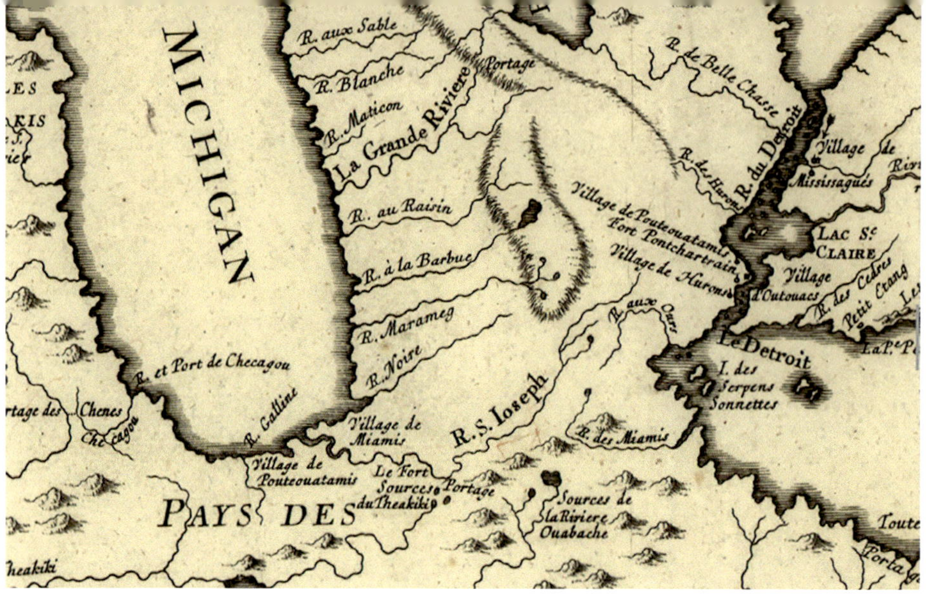

Above: The Bellin 1755 map covering the area from Lake Superior to Kaskaskia and from Delaware Bay to the Mississippi River. It shows a few towns, missions, forts, Indian villages and tribal territory, rivers and lakes, portages, and early place-names. (*Image courtesy of the Library of Congress, Bellin, Jacques Nicolas, and Homann Erben. Partie occidentale de la Nouvelle France ou du Canada. [Nürnberg, 1755] Map. www.loc.gov/item/73694802*)

Below: Lt. Col. William Caldwell, born in Fermanagh, Ireland, around 1750, emigrated to Pennsylvania in 1773. During the American Revolutionary War, he served with the British as captain in the Butler's Rangers at Niagara and Detroit. In 1784, he obtained land near the mouth of the Detroit River and became one of the area's earliest settlers. Christ Church was built in 1819 on land donated by William Caldwell. (*Image courtesy of Susan L. Kelsey*)

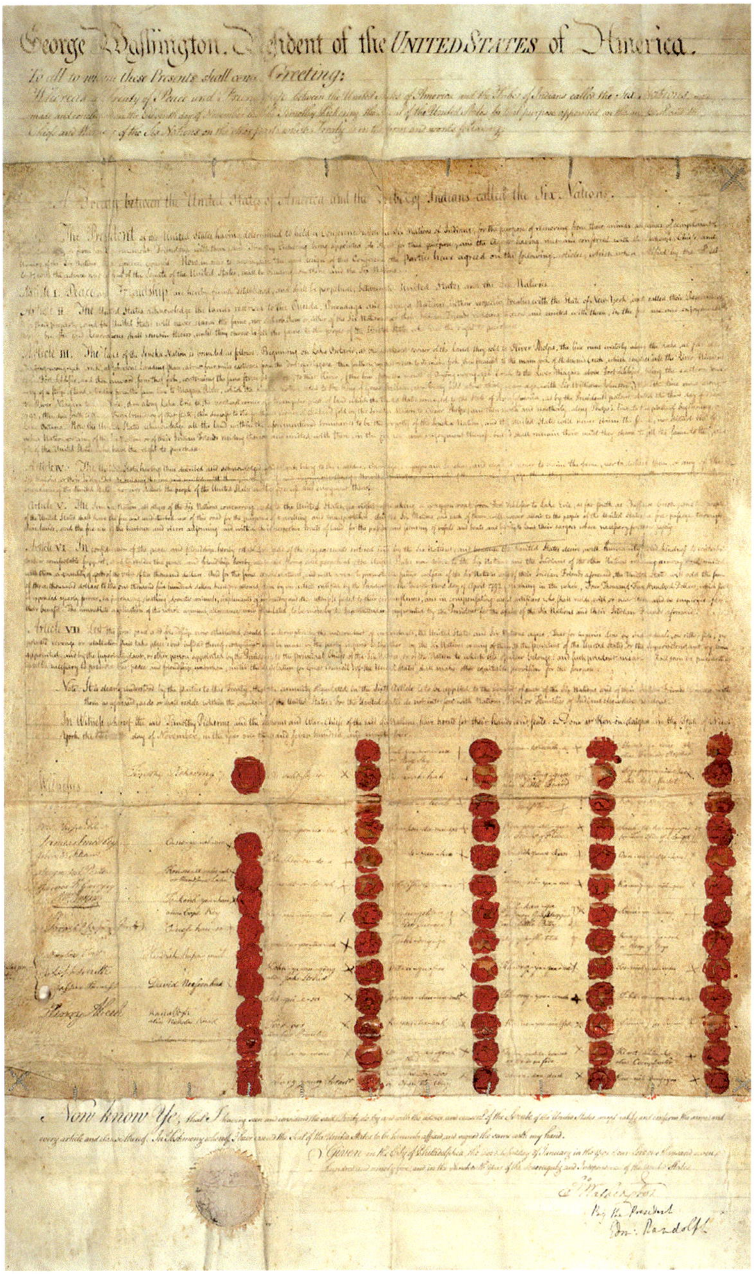

The Treaty of Canandaigua, 1794. One of the earliest treaties between a Native Nation and the United States, it confirmed peace between Six Nations and the United States. The treaty is written on three pieces of parchment stitched together with seals. According to the Library of Congress website, "Nation to Nation: Treaties between the United States and American Indian Nations," each Native delegate signed by drawing an "X" beside his name. President George Washington signed at bottom. (*Image courtesy of the National Museum of the American Indian, Smithsonian Institution, Catalog number 12013254. Photo by NMAI Photo Service*)

This is a silver Treaty of Greenville peace medal, 1795. Caldwell was awarded a medal similar to this. (*Image courtesy of the National Museum of the American Indian, Smithsonian Institution, Catalog number 26/4652. Photo by NMAI Photo Service*)

View of the Detroit River from Amherstburg, Canada. The Detroit River is 28 miles long, 1½–2½ miles wide, and is the international border between the U.S. and Canada. The land across the river is Bois Blanc Island with the City of Detroit just west of the island. (*Image courtesy of Susan L. Kelsey*)

According to the Canadian Government Parks website, Fort Malden was the location of a historic meeting between Major General Sir Isaac Brock and Shawnee Chief Tecumseh, the British stronghold on the Detroit frontier during the War of 1812. Located on the east side of the Detroit River, Amherstburg, Canada. (*Image courtesy of Susan L. Kelsey*)

River. Thirty years later, during an election, the following family names were recorded: Daniel Bourassa, Antoine Ouilmette, Francis LaFramboise, Sr., Francis LaFramboise, Jr., Joseph LaFramboise, Claude LaFramboise, Jean Baptiste Beaubien, Billy Caldwell, and Alexander Robinson. Many of these family names were recorded in Chicago and would follow Caldwell to Missouri, Iowa, and their final removal to Kansas and Oklahoma.

Caldwell began his thirty-seven-year association with John Kinzie (December 23, 1763 to June 6, 1828) and Thomas Forsyth with trading partnerships in 1797, southwest Michigan. Moving between Detroit (east Michigan) and St. Joseph (west Michigan), it was in Detroit that Caldwell started his own fur trading business, working with Kinzie. Caldwell worked on the Wabash River in southeast Detroit after the British exited the Fort Detroit area. Caldwell was educated in a Detroit Jesuit school and moved fluidly between Detroit and the Canadian side of Amherstburg. Kinzie's partner, William Forsyth, was a tavernkeeper in Detroit. Kinzie, born in Canada, moved to Chicago around 1802–03. He was one of the original families in the new fort. The Kinzies built one of the first real residences in Chicago and stayed in the Chicago area until the War of 1812. After his father's death, John Kinzie's mother married William Forsyth. Billy was an instrument to the Scottish men. According to Clifton, these relationships sustained, promoted, and depressed him until the last years of his life. Forsyth would say about Billy: "Billy, you are a kind person, I don't think you would ever hurt a living creature without justification. You always help Indians in need. You are educated and literate and we can use you in our business."

Detroit had around 3,700 people in the late 1700s, mostly residing around the Detroit and St. Clair Rivers. However, the settlement was isolated from civilization. Even Fort Dearborn in Chicago had not yet been built. Kinzie purchased the cabin that had been erected by Pierre LeMai just across the Chicago River from Fort Dearborn.

In 1803, the United States finalized the purchase of the Louisiana territory, acquiring over 530 million acres of new western frontier. Napoleon Bonaparte, needing funds to continue his war with the British, sold the territory for $15 million, which equated to about $0.12 an acre—today worth billions of dollars. In the same decade, the fur trade peaked and demand diminished, resulting in a loss of economy for the Native Americans, contributing to their lack of independence and furthering their need to negotiate for land and annuities.

By 1804, Billy had met Alexander Robinson in Niles, Michigan, and they became lifelong friends. Alexander Robinson, Che-che-bing-way, meaning "blinking eyes," was the son of a Scottish trader and an Ottawa woman. He was born at Mackinaw, Michigan, in 1789. As with many Native Americans, the blending of tribes occurred and Robinson, over time, identified himself as Potawatomi. Caldwell, Robinson, and Shabbona eventually were influential leaders of the Potawatomi, Ottawa, and Ojibwa tribes. During the Treaty of Chicago 1829, Robinson received a reservation on the Des Plaines River where he lived out his life. In 1825, he married a Native American woman, served as an interpreter, spent much time in the Calumet region, and for a time was in the employ of John Jacob Astor. Today, a memorial stone stands on the property located at Lawrence Avenue and River Road in Chicago.

During 1804, Caldwell married his first wife, La Nanette, daughter of White Sturgeon and niece of Mad Sturgeon. La Nanette died giving birth. Caldwell then married the daughter of John Forsyth and an Ojibwa woman, according to James Clifton solidifying

Alexander Robinson (1789–1872), son of an Ottawa mother and a Scots-Irish fur trader father. Robinson was friends with Caldwell and instrumental in the negotiation of the 1833 Treaty of Chicago. (*Image courtesy of Library of Congress. lccn.loc.gov/rc01001871. Kirkland, Joseph, 1830–1894. The Chicago massacre of 1812: with illustrations and historical documents/by Joseph Kirkland. Chicago: Dibble Pub. Co., 1893. 224 p.: ill., facsims, map, ports.; 20 cm E356.C53 K6*)

Alexander Robinson gravesite marked by bolder located at Lawrence and East River Road near the Des Plaines River in Chicago. Located on Cook County Forest Preserve land, the bolder marks the area where Robinson and family members were buried in late 1800s. Dan Melone, archaeologist, discovered the missing headstones and returned them to the Shiller Park Historical Society. Descendants of the Robinson family attended the 2016 ceremony, returning the headstones back to the family. (*Image courtesy of Susan L. Kelsey*)

his business relationship with Kinzie and Forsyth. She also died during childbirth and Caldwell married his third wife, a French woman.

Early Chicago in 1805 was a rough frontier and Indian Country. Caldwell by this time had already had twenty-five years of knowledge about the sweeping white settlements and the future of the Midwest based on his experience with the East Coast. Born shortly after the Revolutionary War, he brought with him the full knowledge and history of the action of an accelerating white settlement growing from the East Coast to the Missouri River.

Native Americans used a long-established game trail around the Great Lakes. The Sauk Trail (also named Michigan Road and the Detroit–Chicago Trail) officially started at the Detroit River. Used by mastodons thousands of years ago, animals made paths through the years, the Native Americans followed the paths, then the stagecoaches followed the paths and, eventually, highways replaced them. In ancient time, buffalo roamed freely in Indian Country and provided a source of food, warmth, and commerce.

The Great Sauk Trail started in Detroit, crossed through Chicago, and later became the Oregon Trail along the Missouri River. In the early 1800s, the Great Sauk Trail was considered the best route between Detroit and Fort Dearborn. It ran through Indian Country, based on the 1821 Chicago Treaty. This trail, called the "Chicago Road," became the main route for settlers moving west. By 1830, pioneer families were heavily using the route.

Buffalo roamed North America until late 1800s where they almost became extinct. Today, buffalo exist in national parks and on reserves. This photo was taken at Badlands National Park, South Dakota. (*Image courtesy of StormCloudsPhotography.com by Laura Hedien*)

Indian trails were the early highways throughout the Great Lakes area. The Sauk Trail connected Detroit with Chicago. Today, many of the modern highways follow the old Indian Trails. (*Image courtesy of Michigan State University Geography Department. geo.msu.edu/extra/geogmich/indian_trails.html*)

The Sauk Trail started in Detroit and continued west through Chicago, across the state of Illinois. This 1903 map highlights several historic locations including the Sauk Trail to Fort Malden, Fort Dearborn, the Des Plaines River, Rock River, Galena, Yellow Banks, and Blackhawk's Village. (*Image courtesy of the Library of Congress, Stevens, Frank Everett, and Alfred Whital Stern Collection Of Lincolniana.. Chicago, Ill., F. E. Stevens, 1903. www.loc.gov/item/03017803/*)

The Great Sauk Trail, replaced by present-day U.S. Highway 112, ran through Ypsilanti, Clinton, Jonesville, Coldwater, Sturgis, White Pigeon, and crossed over the St. Joseph River in western Michigan, past La Porte and Valparaiso in Indiana. From there, it led across Illinois to Rock River and the Mississippi River.

Tanner stated that this era was one of three important periods for the Great Lakes Native Americans. During the early 1800s, Tanner stated it was a historic era in the Great Lakes Indian history. The year 1810 marked the movement of East Coast tribes to the areas of Michigan–Ohio, pushing out existing tribes. The second era was 1830, with the Indian Removal Act. The last era in the 1870s in the Great Lakes region was the battle for resources such as lumber and expansion of the new railroad in high demand. The accelerating westward movements by settlers was unstoppable.

While the American push west for more land and resources took over 200 years, it was the diminishing number of Native Americans that created an inequity. As the white populations grew from the Eastern Seaboard, the Native Americans soon became a minority and had no choice but to leave their land. Today, around 300,000 Native Americans continue to reside in the Great Lakes region.

Based on James A. Clifton's research, Billy was both influenced and disappointed by many of the role models in his life: his father, Joseph Brant, John Kinzie, and Thomas Forsythe. Another man who had lasting influence on Caldwell was Chief Tecumseh, "Panther across the sky." He met Tecumseh through his father and was impressed with Tecumseh's fighting spirit. He would have many interactions with him during the War of 1812.

Billy moved freely across the state of present-day Michigan—at that time, Indian country. He worked with William Burnett, a French trader on the St. Joseph River on the east side of Lake Michigan. Forsyth and Kinzie established a garrison at Chicago for fur trade. This was also an opportunity for Billy to work with his own brother, William. He worked closely with the Fish and Great Sea clans of the Potawatomi tribe. By entering fur trade, he obtained independence, and by the time he was in his twenties, he was a self-managing man.

The St. Joseph area was important to the Great Lakes trail system because it provided a portage between the St. Joseph river and the Kankakee river. The Kankakee river flows into the Illinois river and, eventually, the Mississippi, which then allowed the traveler to go north, south, or cross the river to explore the West. This route has been used for centuries by animals, Native Americans, and the French.

Across the trade routes in Michigan, Caldwell met up with families and individuals that would stay with him the rest of his life. One of those men was Joseph Bertrand from Niles, Michigan. Bertrand, of French descent, possibly born in Canada or Mackinaw, was an early pioneer of southwest Michigan. Bertrand married Madeline, daughter of Chief Topenebee, and established trading posts at the St. Joseph River and on the Sauk Trail.

At the Treaty of Chicago, August 29, 1821, Madeline Bertrand was given one section of land at the Pare aux Vaches. Bertrand's trading post was busy with fur traders on the Detroit–Chicago road. The Bertrand family participated in several treaty negotiations and their children went west to the Potawatomi reserve in Kansas. Bertrand followed about 1858. He died in 1862 and is buried at St. Mary's, Kansas.

According to the Citizen Potawatomi Nation newsletter, *The Hownikan*, around 1755, a French-Canadian named Louis Chevalier established a trading post on the St.

Above: Bi-face projectile points (arrowheads) collected by Edward Gillespie on the former Rouge River in Birmingham, Michigan. The site was near a branch of the Saginaw Indian Trail footpath that connected the Clinton River to the Saginaw Trail. The points are made of Great Lakes chert (flint) between 10,000 B.C. and A.D. 1000. Located at the Michigan Historical Museum. (*Image courtesy of Susan L. Kelsey and the Birmingham Historical Museum and Park*)

Below left: Tecumseh/B.&E. sc.; S.W. (Between 1860 and 1900) photograph. No contemporary portrait of the great chief is known to exist. (*Image courtesy of the Library of Congress, www.loc.gov/item/95509400*)

Below right: Rivers were an important waterway for commerce and transportation. The St. Joseph River in western Michigan allowed for portage between Lake Michigan, the Kankakee River, and the Mississippi River. The image is the Grand River, home to Billy Caldwell in southwestern Canada. (*Image courtesy of Susan L. Kelsey*)

Joseph River. Chevalier was married to a Potawatomi woman and they had a son named Francis or Francois. Francis and his wife had a son named Archange Chevalier. By 1790, Archange married Antoine Ouilmette (Wilmette) and settled at the mouth of the Chicago River. Fur traders by trade, they had eight children: Archange, Elizabeth, Sophie, Joseph, Lewis, Michell, Francis, and Josette. Today, the Chevalier family is recognized with a 338-acre natural preserve along the Des Plaines River in Chicago. It is contiguously connected to the present-day Robinson Reserve, and its history is also connected. Catherine Chevalier was the daughter of the Métis Potawatomi Chief François Pierre Chevalier and Marianne Chevalier. On September 28, 1826, Catherine married Alexander Robinson. These reserves were a result of the Treaty of 1829 and encompassed over 600 acres. Robinson Woods contains the remains of the Robinson homestead and a small cemetery where Catherine, Alexander, and their children are buried. Archeologist Dan Melone discovered the long-lost tombstones of the Robinson family; they are located at the Robinson Heritage Preservation Collective at the Shiller Park Historical Commission at the Shiller Park Public Library. Descendants of Robinson live in the area still today.

Another family inextricably connected to Billy Caldwell is the LaFramboise family: Joseph LaFramboise, son of François, and his Potawatomi wife. Shaw-we-no-qua was born around 1798 near the St. Joseph River in Michigan. According to Find-a-grave, he had three wives and fourteen children. He became a Potawatomi chief by marriage to Therese Peltier. LaFramboise, with Caldwell, Robinson, and Shabbona, acted as one of the principal spokesmen for the Prairie and Lake Potawatomi at the Chicago Treaty of 1833. For that, he received $300 for a claim at the treaty in September, plus $1,000 for his children, and was granted an annuity of $200 per year for life, as well as one section of land on the Des Plaines River immediately south of the northern Indian boundary line for himself and his six children, located on the present-day Indian Boundary Division of the Forest Preserve District of Cook County. Joseph died in February 1867 in Silver Lake, Shawnee County, Kansas—a location that will reveal information about what happened after Billy Caldwell died in 1841.

In present-day Niles, Michigan, a Fort St. Joseph archeological project is taking place to unearth historic clues to the former Fort St. Joseph. This is a collaboration between Western Michigan University (W.M.U.) faculty and students, the City of Niles, and the Fort St. Joseph Archaeology Advisory Committee. The curation of the collections ensures that the artifacts and associated documentation are preserved for public education.

As the trails lead west to an emerging Chicago, remnants of the trails can still be seen today.

Joseph La Framboise, friend of Caldwell, was chief of the Potawatomi Tribe following the death of Caldwell in Council Bluffs, Iowa. He fought in the Blackhawk War of 1832 and served as an interpreter throughout his life. Later, after the death of Caldwell, he signed the 1861 Iowa Treaty, moving his tribe to Kansas, home of present-day Prairie Band Potawatomi Nation. He is buried in the Silver Lake Cemetery in Shawnee County, Silver Lake, Kansas. Featured image Indian Agency House, U.S. Route 1, Silver Lake, Shawnee County, KS. This stone house, said to be a former Indian Agency building, is perhaps the earliest structure built by white men still standing in Kansas. Structure dates *c.* 1826–*c.* 1827 initial construction. (*Image courtesy of the Library of Congress, www.loc.gov/item/ks0038/*)

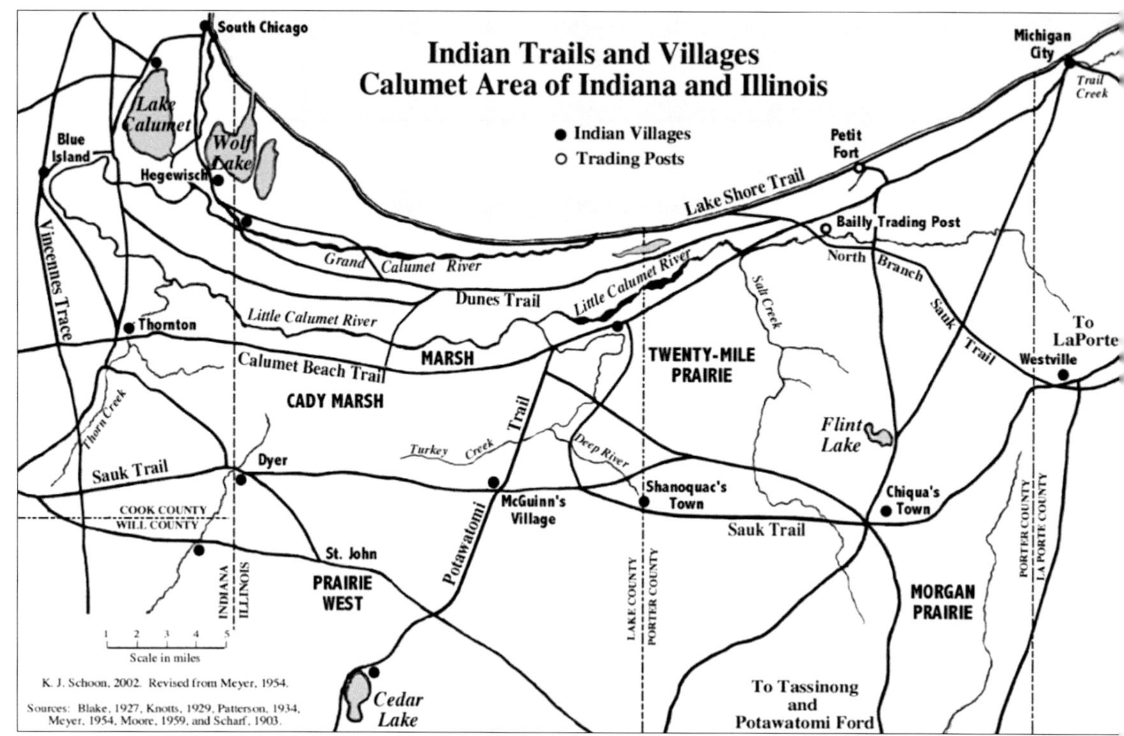

Indian Trails south of Lake Michigan with the vastness of trade business and commerce around the Great Lakes. (*Image courtesy of Ken Schoon, University of Indiana Press*)

4

1805: A Frontier in Transition

No river can return to its source, yet all rivers must have a beginning.

Tribe unknown

In the Chicago area, the Wisconsin glacier retreated around 15,000 years ago. Chicago indigenous people are documented as early as 12,000 years ago, French explorers, traders, and missionaries followed shortly after. While Detroit already had a fort by at least 100 years, Chicago, "Chicagou," emerged as a trading post around the early 1700s. Following the end of the French and Indian War (1763), the Chicago region still had French residents, but under English rule, until July 4, 1776.

In 1803, the United States built Fort Dearborn on the south side of the Chicago River. The fort was built by Captain Whistler and named in honor of Captain Dearborn, U.S. Secretary of War. This fort was located on the Chicago River, behind a sandbar on the edge of Lake Michigan. Today, brass plates are visible on sidewalks located at the intersection of Michigan Avenue and Wacker Drive, outlining the fort walls. The first resident of present-day Chicago was Jean Baptiste Point Du Sable, around 1779. His cabin was located on the north bank of Chicago River near its mouth and the point where it turned south just before meeting the lake. In 1796, Du Sable sold his cabin to a French trader, Le Mai (referred to Chicago by St. Joseph's Bennett). By 1804, John Kinzie purchased the cabin.

During this era, the fur trade was the main economic activity of Chicago. Fort Dearborn was established to protect the American fur interest. A variety of companies were operating in the Great Lakes region: the North West Company (1779), mostly on Lake Superior; the Michilimackinac Company, out of Mackinac, worked Lake Michigan and the Mississippi River; and the American Fur Company (1808), established by John Jacob Astor, competed with the existing Canadian Hudson Bay Company. As a fur agent, Kinzie worked the Chicago area and reported to Mackinac Island. Families

Old Fort Dearborn, 1803–1812, from a sketch by Charles H. Ourand, based upon plans drawn by Capt. J. Whistler, 1808. (*Image courtesy of the Chicago History Museum, ICHi-003038*)

already referenced in this book, including Beaubien and Hubbard, also assisted Kinzie and eventually bought the business from him. By the 1820s, Astor dominated the Chicago fur trade.

Fort Dearborn, erected at the mouth of the Chicago River, was also built for defense against the Native Americans. It stood on the south side of the Chicago River, had two blockhouses, and was near the entrance of the Chicago River and Lake Michigan. Built from locally-sourced wood, soon other buildings housing artillery and supplies were built nearby. Some 3 miles south of the fort was Hardscrabble, present-day Bridgeport.

Although the 1795 Treaty of Greenville had already ceded millions of acres around the mouth of the Chicago River, thousands of Potawatomi and other tribes still lived around the southern Lake Michigan region.

Albert F. Scharf, historian and cartographer, mapped out Indian Trails and Villages of Chicago around 1804. This detailed map showcases the existing Indian villages north of Fort Dearborn and along the Illinois Des Plaines River. Included in this wonderful map are major/minor Indian villages, chipping stations along the river, portage sites, natural spring water, signal stations (at geographic high locations), Indian mounds, effigy mounds, and trails.

A closer look at the inset map outlines two major 1804 Indian camps in the general area of the 1833 Billy Caldwell reservation. The camps are located along the Chicago North Branch River, with access to portage further south in present-day Portage Park, Chicago.

An 1804 map drawn by Albert F. Scharf detailing Indian trails and villages in the Chicago area. (*Image courtesy of the Chicago History Museum, ICHi-031997*)

Kinzie home on the Chicago River around early 1800s. John Kinzie became known as "The Father of Chicago." Starting as an employee of the American Fur Company, he was an Indian trader and garrison of Fort Dearborn. (*Image courtesy of the Susan L. Kelsey postcard collection*)

A detailed Scharf map insert shows the present-day communities of Forest Glen, Sauganash, and Edgebrook and the historic Indian villages that were located next to the north branch of the Chicago River. (*Courtesy of the Chicago History Museum, ICHi-031997*)

Using Scharf's 1804 map of Indian Trails and Villages of Chicago, long before Billy Caldwell was awarded his 1,600-acre reservation, major Potawatomi Indian villages existed in the same area (current-day Edgebrook, Sauganash, and Forest Glen). The Chicago north branch was a major transportation route with direct access to Fort Dearborn and portage to the Des Plaines River. Native Americans preferred the interior rivers to the unpredictable and cold Lake Michigan. These villages were outside the Fort Dearborn 1816 "boundary line" that extended from the fort, south of Sauganash, and along the southeastern edge of Edgebrook. Indian Country was comprised of natural waterways, foot trails, an abundance of wildlife, and prairie grass.

Illinois land surveyors (1849) used the Indian boundaries lines, trail marker trees, and campsites in their survey notes.

A year after Fort Dearborn was built, on May 18, 1804, John Kinzie came to Chicago. Building on his Detroit business, he negotiated the complex social and economic world. Born in Quebec in 1763, Kinzie moved to Detroit as a boy after his widowed mother married Thomas Forsyth, a Scots-Irish merchant at Grosse Point, Michigan. Kinzie married Margaret Mackenzie, but after the revolution, Margaret returned to Virginia with their three children and Kinzie was married a second time, to Elizabeth McPhillip—a Detroit widow politically connected to local tribes. Kinzie continued trading in Michigan, but after 1803, he relocated to Chicago where he traded with the surrounding Native American communities. He built a new trading post on the south side of the river, near the newly established Fort Dearborn, and supplied the garrison with both luxuries and necessities.

By 1810, settlement at Chicago clustered at several places. North of the river's mouth were the Kinzie family whose patriarch, John A. Kinzie, occupied DuSable's old mansion. Further north, at Grosse Pointe (Wilmette), Antoine Ouilmette and his relatives maintained a trading post where the road to Milwaukee launched from Chicago north to other trading posts. On the south side of the river, near Fort Dearborn, Jean Baptiste Beaubien and his family maintained a trading establishment and occupied a series of log houses. Further south was Hardscrabble (modern Bridgeport), where the southern branch of the river emerged from Mud Lake. Alexander Robinson, members of the Bourassa, LaFramboise, and Chevalier families and other families close to Caldwell during his time in Michigan, all lived in Chicago. To the west, along the Des Plaines in modern-day Riverside, several villages of Potawatomi's had erected their cabins and wigwams.

Kinzie's ascension at Chicago continued the pattern of white traders married to Native American (or captive) women. As Kinzie's trading establishment grew, he employed large numbers of Métis including Billy Caldwell and Alexander Robinson from Michigan. Moreover, he also cemented his ties with Métis traders at Milwaukee, apprenticing their part-Potawatomi children as servants or employees in his household. Yet, by 1800, the Indian trade at Chicago was no longer financed by, or dependent upon, traders at Peoria or southern Illinois. Its new ties were to Mackinac and Detroit, and trading houses at those locations supplied the Chicago community with most of its goods and finances. Moreover, the Great Sauk Trail, an overland route between the upper Mississippi Valley and British Indian Department offices in Ontario, passed just south of Chicago, providing additional ties between Kinzie and other traders with merchants at Detroit or in Canada.

Land surveyors would use Indian Trail Marker Trees as reference points. Old field notes included trail marker trees, geographical landmarks, campsites, rivers, and other historical markers to indicate boundary lines. (*Image courtesy of Dennis Downes*)

Chicago in 1831, with views of Fort Dearborn and homes of John Dean, J. Baptiste Beaubien, Dr. Wolcott, and John Kinzie. (*Image courtesy of the Library of Congress, Chicago with views of Fort Dearborn and homes of John Dean, J. Baptiste Beaubien, Dr. Wolcott and John Kinzie*, c. *1897. Aug. 31. Photograph. www.loc.gov/item/2004680484*)

Caldwell was the chief clerk in the Forsythe-Kinzie firm's new post at the mouth of the Chicago River. In his territory, he would have covered Chicago up to Milwaukee, the Menominee's Rock River, the Winnebago's Illinois River, and the Potawatomi's Kankakee River in Sangamon County. Forsythe's business had pack horses, equipment, boats, and canoes. Most of the furs were brought to Chicago on pack horses; boats would come in spring and fall bringing supplies and goods in exchange for the pelts. The furs would be shipped to Mackinac, a depot of John Astor's American Fur Company. The fort would have been a lively place with the presence of voyagers, usually French-Canadian, employed by fur companies. Caldwell was a clerk for Kinzie at the time and would have traded with Mackinac traders to secure tobacco and pipes, needles and thread, and bright ribbons in exchange for skins to make moccasins.

Caldwell married into the Potawatomi tribe; his in-laws called him Sauganash (Englishman). He was married at least four times. His first marriage was to La Nanette in 1804, daughter of Nee-scot-nee-meg, one of the most famous chiefs of the nation. La Nanette died shortly after their marriage; they had one child named Alexander. La Nanette was the niece of Potawatomi Chief Mad Sturgeon. His second wife was the daughter of his employer, Robert Forsyth, and an Ojibwa woman, who died soon after

John Kinzie home on the edge of the Chicago River. From 1804 to 1812, a few log cabins were occupied by traders. During the War of 1812, many left the area and returned in the fall of 1816. (*Image courtesy of Chicago History Museum, ICHi-038122*)

marriage. On November 18, 1834, Caldwell married Saqua (Sangua) Le Grand and she went with him to Iowa. The *Illinois Catholic Historical Review* (1918) states William Caldwell married Susanna Misnakwe on January 2, 1839 by Father De Smet in Council Bluffs, Iowa.

Kinzie's home was located across the river from Fort Dearborn and provided his family with a strategic location on the edge of Lake Michigan.

By 1810, the pattern of relationship between the white settlers and the Native Americans had been set in the region, and the spheres of influence revolved around fur trading, Métis, the natural resources around Lake Michigan and the Great Lakes. This new pattern would impact Caldwell's life from here forward.

5

1812: Panther Across the Sky

It is no longer good enough to cry peace, we must act peace, live peace and live in peace.

Shenandoah

Prior to the War of 1812, a geological phenomenon occurred—starting late 1811 and continuing into the early months of 1812. At 2:15 a.m. on December 16, 1811, the New Madrid earthquake shook the ground with a magnitude of 7.5, originating from New Madrid, Missouri. Ground vibrations were felt as far north as Canada and south to the Gulf, encompassing thousands of miles. A second quake over 7.5 was felt again on January 23, 1812, and a third quake over 7.5 on February 11, 1812, with over 2,000 aftershocks. With the country already in a sweeping cultural change, the apocalyptic series of earthquakes were a spiritual element for both the white and the Native American populations. Tecumseh and his brother, Tenskwatawa ("The Prophet"), were influential leaders during this time period. Tecumseh, also known as "Panther across the sky," was at his pinnacle of leadership in the pan-Indian Nation. Adding to the phenomenon was a visible comet that started earlier in March 1811 and was visible for 260 days. Named Napoleon's Comet by Europeans, and Tecumseh's Comet by Americans, it preceded the New Madrid earthquake. Tecumseh, Chief of the Shawnees, predicted the earthquakes as part of his prophecy.

On the political front, two conflicts were going on during this time—one between Americans and the British, and the second between Americans and the Indians. In the American-British conflict, there were more than sixteen major actions, with the Battle of the Thames being a significant one. In the American-Indian conflict, there were four major actions with the Chicago Battle of Fort Dearborn on August 1812 as a major event.

In June 1812, Tecumseh shifted his war headquarters to south of Fort Malden, on Indian Agent Matthew Elliott's farm. Caldwell's father, William Caldwell, was captain of Butler's Rangers at that time. Billy Caldwell, thirty-two years of age during this war,

New Madrid Earthquake. The aftermath of the earthquakes in New Madrid, Missouri, 1811–12. Wood engraving, nineteenth century. (*Image courtesy of Granger, NYC*)

worked closely with his father and Tecumseh during this period. In July, Tecumseh organized 150 Indians and militia, intimidating General William Hull at Fort Detroit, and the fort fell to the British on August 15, 1812. Billy's brother, William, was at Detroit during this time. This action, combined with the Fall of Fort Michilimackinac a few weeks earlier, brazened the Native Americans for a short time—until the end of the War of 1812.

The Fall of Fort Michilimackinac (July 17, 1812), which controlled the important straits of Mackinaw and Fort Detroit (August 16, 1812), and access to the eastern Great Lakes occurred around the same time as the Battle of Fort Dearborn. Slow communications during that era made it difficult to gauge reliable information.

Although Chicago was a young outpost on the frontier, elsewhere, the battles for sovereignty were raging. On August 9, 1812, a young Indian runner, Winnemac, brought Detroit General Hull's order to Fort Dearborn instructing Captain Heald to evacuate the fort. A terrific painting by artist Hal Sherman interprets the meeting between Brock, Tecumseh, Billy Caldwell, and Commander of the Caldwell Rangers William Caldwell (left to right). Available to view at www.uppercanadahistory.ca/brock/brock5.html.

Six days later, Captain Heald evacuated the fort and was ambushed by 500 Natives at the present-day intersection of Prairie Avenue and 18th Street, Chicago. The Battle of Fort Dearborn was one of the opening battles of the War of 1812.

According to Ann Durkin Keating, *Rising Up from Indian Country*, Chicago was on the periphery of the Washington, D.C., war debate, and news took weeks to travel west

Photo of Captain William Caldwell (sitting far left), assumed to be brother of Billy Caldwell (son of Suzanne Baby Caldwell). (*Image courtesy of the Marsh Historical Collection, Amherstburg, Ontario Canada*)

An 1812 Chicago map featuring Ouilmette's home, the Agency House, the Chicago River, and Fort Dearborn on the south side of the river. (*Image courtesy of Chicago Historical Museum*)

Fort Dearborn postcard from the World's Fair showcasing the blockhouse and soldier's barracks during the 1933 Century of Progress World's Fair and Chicago's pioneer history. (*Postcard courtesy of the Susan L. Kelsey private collection*)

across the country. But in Chicago, Kinzie, Forsyth, Caldwell, and many other traders had complex relationships based on business and family connections. News was not always timely or accurate and left families to decipher information and make decisions about their family's safety and future.

On August 15, 1812, a nine-year-old John H. Kinzie, son of John A. Kinzie, was taken from Fort Dearborn by boat over to the St. Joseph River in western Michigan with other Kinzie family members. They were escorted by Alexander Robinson to the Bertrand home in St. Joseph. Some 148 men, women, and children lost their lives, with additional losses by Native Americans in the battle. The Battle of Fort Dearborn is well-documented in numerous resources.

Following the Battle of Fort Dearborn, Caldwell and his friends, Alexander Robinson, Shabbona, and others, travelled back and forth from Chicago to Michigan. The War of 1812 continued with intense wars on October 5, 1813 at the Battle of the Thames, near Moraviantown (present-day Ontario, Canada). Tecumseh and General Proctor advanced toward the Thames River with more than 3,000 Indians, 900 British troops, plus 290 more Indians—close to 5,000 total. U.S. General William Henry Harrison, Governor of Ohio and future U.S. President, led the battle in Moraviantown, forcing the retreat of Indian and British forces.

Tecumseh ("Flying Panther"), Chief of the Shawnees, brave leader of Indians and brother of Tenskwatawa ("The Prophet") was born about March 1768. Tecumseh was a comrade of Billy's father and Billy would have known of him as a child. Tecumseh would visit

Burning of Fort Dearborn in 1812. The fort was rebuilt in 1816. (*Postcard courtesy of the Susan L. Kelsey private collection*)

Above left: Battle of Fort Dearborn, 1812, also known as the Chicago Massacre. (*Postcard courtesy of the Susan L. Kelsey private collection*)

Above right: The death of Tecumseh at the Battle of Thames, October 5, 1813. (Image courtesy of the Library of Congress, Death of Tecumseh. Battle of the Thames, Oct. 5th,/ J. L. McGee, del et lith. [New York: N. Currier] Photograph. Retrieved from the Library of Congress, <www.loc.gov/item/2007683559>)

with the senior Caldwell at his home in Amherstburg. Tecumseh was younger than Billy's father, but twelve years older than Billy and served as a mentor and, later in life, a friend. Tecumseh worked closely with senior Caldwell and the British, leading battles in many towns around Detroit. Billy would have been around thirty-two years old during this battle and was described as 6 feet tall, 155 lb., lean, active, a runner, and multi-lingual—speaking English, French, Potawatomi, and some Mohawk. Tecumseh fought next to Blue Jacket, brother of Billy's mother, Rising Sun. Billy Caldwell became a confidant of Tecumseh, eventually witnessing his death on October 5, 1813 at the Battle of the Thames.

Tecumseh had created a pan-Indian confederacy to stop Anglo-Americans from seizing American Indian land. In 1810 and 1811, Tecumseh tried to unite all the tribes in a pan-Indian confederation to stop Americans from taking land and advancing. Tecumseh was killed on October 5, 1831, marking the end of his confederacy.

To this day, the location of the remains of Tecumseh are unknown. The Indian spirit was broken until the 1832 Blackhawk wars. The death of Tecumseh was a defining moment in the life of Billy Caldwell and for all natives in Indian Country. It was at that point that they realized they did not have the support of Great Britain and that they would lose their land and their way of life forever. Today, over fifteen cities or towns are named after Tecumseh.

Early on, notes from the Draper Manuscript provided personal accounts and details about Caldwell and Tecumseh. Benjamin Drake and his brother, Daniel Draper, collected notes on Tecumseh from about 1863 until Draper's death.

In June 1816, Fort Malden ceased rations to Indians. Caldwell's letter to Canadian William Claus, Indian Affairs, states: "Sir, if I was back again in 1811 and knew as much as I know now, I assure you I would take care of my own affairs and not get into political affairs again."

Almost immediately after the War of 1812, Native Americans ceded nearly 18 million acres of land from Detroit to the Mississippi River. By 1816, Fort Dearborn was rebuilt on the site of the 1812 fort.

Billy Caldwell, still formally aligned with the British Army, sent a letter to William Claus, Canadian Indian Affairs (courtesy of Marsh Collections, Amherstburg, Ontario):

> The last testimony I have to offer to the Country where my father won his living is to exert its utmost endeavor to nciliate [*sic.*] the remaining nations (of Indians) who consider themselves greatly neglected by people who profess their friendship. Although the poor Indians did receive the annual presents, it is poor payment for the extensive untry [*sic.*] which they ceded to the English when the French withdrew from this country. What I have written here is not with a view to bread, but merely to put you in mind of a future day as you at the head of the department. Billy Caldwell, Detroit Indian department, 1816

In 1818, Illinois became a state and changes accelerated in the Midwest region of the Great Lakes.

Following the war, Caldwell, Sr., conducted business across the border between Detroit and Fort Malden. In 1818, he drew up his will leaving his property only to his legitimate children, leaving Billy Caldwell without property or a future career. Soon after, Billy Caldwell moved to Chicago forever.

Above left: Print shows Tecumseh shielding prisoners from another Native American on horseback wielding a tomahawk during the War of 1812; another Native is about to scalp a dead soldier. (*Image courtesy of the Library of Congress, Virtue, Emmins & Co., Publisher. Tecumseh Saving Prisoners. N.Y.: Virtue & Co., Publishers. Photograph. www.loc.gov/item/2012645310*)

Above right: Location of the Battle of Thames, Ontario, Canada. Great Shawnee Chief and Warrior Tecumseh died during the War of 1812. The image shows Tecumseh shielding prisoners from another Native American on horseback wielding a tomahawk during the War of 1812; another Native is about to scalp a dead soldier. (*Image courtesy of the Library of Congress, Virtue, Emmins & Co., Publisher. Tecumseh Saving Prisoners. United States, c. 1860. N.Y.: Virtue & Co., Publishers. Photograph. www.loc.gov/item/2012645310*)

Below: Reoccupied Fort Dearborn 1816, second Fort Dearborn. The new fort was a square stockade with officers' quarters, barracks, magazine, and provision house. The Chicago government agency was connected with Billy Caldwell, interpreter; David McKee, blacksmith; and Joseph Porthier, striker. (*Postcard courtesy of the Susan L. Kelsey private collection*)

Above: By 1818, Illinois became a state and the east United States was taking shape with the western half of the United States still frontier and Indian Country. (*Map courtesy of Melish, John, et al. United States of America. Philadelphia: Murray, Draper, Fairman & Co, 1818. Map. Retrieved from the Library of Congress, www.loc.gov/item/2002621136/. www.loc.gov/resource/g3700.ct003955/?r=0.241,0.246,0.557,0.214,0*)

Below: Image of Chicago 1820, featuring Fort Dearborn on the south (left) side of the Chicago River and the Kinzie home on the north (right) side of the river. The Chicago river was originally about 40 yards wide. Previously, the river turned southward to about present-day Madison street. In 1825, Chicago contained about fourteen homes. (*Image courtesy of the Library of Congress, Chicago Lithographing Co. Chicago 1867, www.loc.gov/item/2009633650*)

By 1821, the Treaty of Chicago was signed. It was the first major treaty since 1807 and set the pattern for things to come. According to Keating, treaties developed a regular structure with four parts. The first part was a declaration of peace between the parties. The second described the details of the cession of the land. The third part detailed the money and annuities and the fourth allowed for specific conditions.

Billy held various positions in the emerging territory—Justice of the Peace in 1825 at the age of forty-three and Peoria Election Commissioner in 1826 at the age of forty-four. Reading early election records sounds like current-day Chicago politics, as family names are the same and dynasties are passed down generationally. John Kinzie was commissioned Justice of the Peace on July 28, 1825. His son-in-law, Alexander Wolcott, and Jean Baptiste Beaubien were commissioned on September 10, 1825. Judges in 1826 were John Kinzie, Jean B. Beaubien, and Billy Caldwell. The clerks were Archibald Clybourne and John K. Clark. The Indian Agent was Dr. Alexander Wolcott—the son-in-law of John Kinzie. Billy Caldwell was living in Chicago with a total of five people listed on a petition of the Catholics of Chicago to Bishop Rosati, along with the names of Beaubien, LaFramboise, Pothier, Alex Robinson, Ouilmette, Bourassa, and Chevalier. Many of these family members and friends would follow him to Council Bluffs, Iowa.

The 1825, an engineering marvel created the Erie Canal, allowing Easterners to easily travel and relocate west on the new frontier.

Erie Canal commemorative pitcher. In Chicago, five different (future I&M Canal) canal routes were surveyed and costs estimated. The highest estimate was $716,110. Chicago wanted water communication with New York via the Great Lakes and Erie Canal. (*Image courtesy of the Susan L. Kelsey private collection*)

In 1826, Mark Beaubien, an early pioneer, half Indian and half French, bought a log cabin on the southeast corner of Lake Street and Wacker Drive, then the property of John Kinzie, and converted it into a tavern. In 1830, he added a second floor and named it the Sauganash Hotel, in honor of Billy Caldwell. The hotel was a place where settlers and officers mixed with natives and decided the events of the territory. According to research, the hotel was a wild place with dancing, drinking, Indian maidens, sleeping on porches, and wrestling matches on the front lawn. At this time, there were twelve families living in the territory. In a period of three years, that number swelled to 550 families.

In 1828, the U.S. Indian Department built a wood frame house for Caldwell, located near present-day State Street and Chicago Avenue. The timbers were from the land north of the house and the brick was brought from Cleveland, Ohio.

By 1829, Billy Caldwell was named Chief Sauganash, leader of the Potawatomi tribes. The Native Americans knew it was only a matter of time before the whites would move into the Great Lakes states, so they allowed Billy Caldwell (Chief Sauganash), Chief Shabbona, and Chief Alexander Robinson to represent them in the final 1829 treaty. By 1827, it was evident that America was determined to expand west. The Treaty of Prairie du Chien was signed in 1829 and American miners rushed to the lead mining area of northern Illinois and southwest Wisconsin, encompassing Indian country. Within eight years, the Potawatomi lost 70 percent of their land and were reduced to small reservations, making it impossible to support themselves.

The Treaty of the Prairie du Chien in 1829 was one the last treaties. The meeting was held at Prairie du Chien, Wisconsin. There were over 13,300 men, women, and children present along with tribe agents and interpreters. Billy Caldwell was recognized as the Chief of United Nations. After two days of negotiations, the treaty was signed and ratified in Congress on January 2, 1830. In the treaty, Billy Caldwell was granted two and a half sections of land on the Chicago River, around 1,600 acres above the Line of Purchase of 1816. This is located at the present-day intersection of I-94 and Peterson/Caldwell Road in North Chicago. Alexander Robinson, Chief of the United Potawatomi, Chippewa, and Ottawa, was granted two sections of land on the reservation along the Des Plaines River. Around the 1830s, Father Badin baptized three of Billy Caldwell's children on the 1,600-acre reserve. The image is depicted in the present-day Queen of All Saints Basilica windows in the Sauganash neighborhood on the north side of Chicago.

By 1830, the regional pressure to remove Native Americans from the growing white areas was unstoppable. There were several factors that drove this pressure. The Erie Canal, started in 1825, made the movement from the east down the St. Lawrence River to the Great Lakes easy. Navigation was made easier in 1818 with steam engines. The Indian Removal Act (1830) forced Native Americans to leave their homelands and move, like the mastodons thousands of years earlier.

James Bucklin, Chief Engineer of the Illinois & Michigan Canal, came in 1830 to survey. According to the Wentworth papers (Newberry Library), it was Caldwell who had explained and suggested the canal would make a feeder of the Calumet River. The survey was started in 1830, which linked the Great Lakes with the Mississippi River and the Gulf of Mexico by the building of a new I&M Canal. Chief Shabbona was hired for his expertise since he lived at Paw Paw Grove, around 70 miles west of Chicago.

As Fergus stated, the development of the I&M Canal enabled early Chicagoans to profit from the growing new city: "Taking advantage of the low prices at which, the Canal property sold, they purchased, and having the sagacity, some of them, to hold onto their purchase, they increased in value upon their hands, and made them rich." Like present-day Chicago, political D.N.A. is truly in the soil of the Chicago Great Lakes region.

On August 2, 1830, at the home of James Kinzie, the first election precinct of Peoria County was held. Polled in the vote were Jonathan N. Bailey (first postmaster), John B. Beaubien, Medore B. Beaubien (later moved to Kansas), Leon Bourassa, James Brown, Billy Caldwell (Indian Chief), Jean Baptiste Chevalier, John L. Davis, James Kinzie, Joseph LaFramboise, Stephen Mack (clerk of the American Fur Company), Rev. Jesse Walker from Peoria, Mark Beaubien, and others.

By 1830, the population in the new America was more than 12 million people. Some of the first wagon trains left on the Oregon Trail. Cyrus H. McCormick invented the reaper in Virginia and eventually became a local Chicago legend. Geronimo, leader of the Bedonkohe band of the Chiricahua Apache tribe and Sitting Bull, a Hunkpapa Lakota holy man, had just been born and they would lead the last of the Native American fights in the western territories until the late 1800s.

The year 1831 brought a new stagecoach to Chicago. Galena had emerged as an important lead-mining town and "Indian territory" was officially west of the Mississippi. Concurrently, a new wave of religious conversation was starting by the Protestants and Catholic missionaries to convert Native Americans. The fur trade was rapidly declining, thereby reducing income to Native Americans, making the federal annuities and land a new way to survive and provide for their families. Native Americans negotiated for sovereignty and annuities in exchange of their lands and removal from their homeland.

By 1832, Fort Dearborn was reoccupied by Major William Whistler. At the same time, the last Indian battle of the area was led by Chief Blackhawk of the Sauk tribe. He led 2,000 Sauks across the Mississippi from his holding place in Iowa and started the Blackhawk War to rid the Great Lakes of white men.

Billy Caldwell, Shabbona, and Alexander Robinson were against Blackhawk's efforts, would not join him, and, in fact, tried to talk him out of battle. With the 1832 Blackhawk War, Shabbona volunteered his services, even though many of the settlers had treated him poorly. In February 1832, a council of chiefs from the Sauk, Fox, Winnebago, and Potawatomi tribes was held and lasted for many days and nights. Eloquent appeals were made to fight the encroaching white people. Blackhawk's position was that this was the last opportunity to fight for Indian Country before it was too late. Only one tribe joined Blackhawk, with the rest of the Potawatomi and other tribes joining Shabbona and Sauganash.

Since the death of Tecumseh, Shabbona had acted as missionary for peace among the Indians. In the fall of 1832, Shabbona warned whites, was considered a traitor to Blackhawk, and was not allowed to attend any future Indian councils. He rode for over forty-eight hours. In fact, he rode his pony to death, removed the saddle, and rode another pony to warn white settlers about the impending attack by Blackhawk. On May 21, 1832, Blackhawk massacred white settlers at Indian Creek, 12 miles north of modern-day Ottawa.

Blackhawk and the Prophet, representing the Sauk and Fox Nations, met in early 1832 to prevent the further encroachment of the white settlers. Caldwell and Shabbona argued against the fight, suggesting that the loss of life was too great for Native Americans.

On July 21, 1832, Blackhawk led Sauk and Fox tribes in one of the last Midwest American-Indian battles near present-day Sauk City, Wisconsin. Angered by the loss of

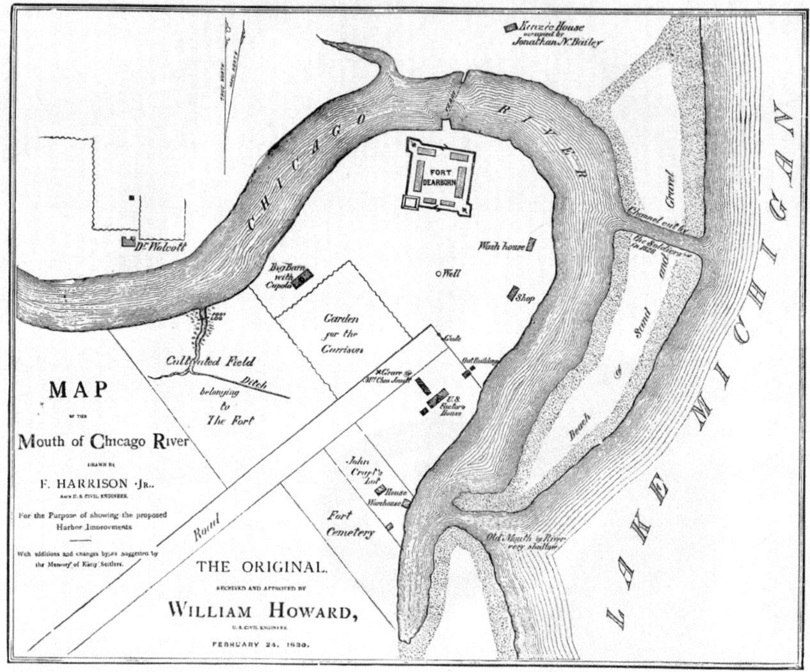

Above: An 1830 map of Chicago at the mouth of Chicago River and Lake Michigan. Map features Fort Dearborn, fort cemetery, Dr. Wolcott's home, barns, warehouses, wash house, garden, Kinzie House at the top of the map, and harbor improvements. (*Map courtesy of the Chicago History Museum, ICHi-021558*)

Below: Chicago in 1831, with views of Fort Dearborn and homes of John Dean, J. Baptiste Beaubien, Dr. Wolcott, and John Kinzie. (*Image courtesy of the Library of Congress, Chicago with views of Fort Dearborn and homes of John Dean, J. Baptiste Beaubien, Dr. Wolcott and John Kinzie, c. 1897. Aug. 31. Photograph. www.loc.gov/item/2004680484*)

Above left: Blackhawk War 1832, last great Indian war in the Great Lakes region. This image was from the historic battle site near Sauk City, Wisconsin. Another great exhibit is located at Hauberg Indian Museum, a collection by Dr. John Hauberg, a Rock Island philanthropist in Rock Island, IL. (*Image courtesy of Susan L. Kelsey*)

Above right: Image of Sauk Chief Blackhawk from the Frank Everett Stevens and Alfred Whital Stern Collection Of Lincolniana. The book includes a review of Blackhawk's life, the Blackhawk war, and illustrated with upward of 300 rare and interesting portraits and views. (*Image courtesy of the Library of Congress, www.loc.gov/item/03017803/*)

Right: Wisconsin Heights' battlefield located near present-day Sauk City, Wisconsin. (*Image courtesy of Susan L. Kelsey*)

his birthplace, Blackhawk led a fierce battle against the U.S. militia. Blackhawk escaped over the Mississippi River.

Sixty Sauk warriors held off 700 troops under Henry Dodge while Blackhawk's band crossed the Wisconsin River. The site of the Wisconsin Heights Battlefield is the only intact site of the American Indian Wars left in the Midwest. The three-month war ended in a massacre at the Battle of Bad Axe on August 2, 1832.

In late 1832, Blackhawk was captured and imprisoned until April 1833, when he moved to live on the Iowa River and died in 1838.

According to Tanner, "the war demoralized the members of Sauk tribe. By 1836, all Indian lands in northern Illinois and southern Wisconsin had been ceded, clearing them for American occupancy. The Black Hawk War broke surviving Indian resistance to American domination of the Great Lakes region."

As the Blackhawk War was winding down, the town of Chicago was adding new residents daily. The Sauganash Hotel, also known as Sauganash Tavern, was located at present-day southeast corner of Lake Street and Wacker Drive. Built in 1831 by Mark Beaubien as a tavern, it was named after Billy Caldwell and was the social hotel and center of the young Chicago. The Beaubien original log cabin was enlarged with clapboard siding and blue shutters. On August 10, 1833, the town's first trustees were elected there. The hotel was destroyed by fire in 1851. The first frame house in Cook County was built in 1818 by the Government for Billy Caldwell. It stood on Superior Street, but was later moved to Indiana, west of Cass.

The Blackhawk War was over, Chicago was growing as a new town on the edge of the new frontier, and change was accelerating in the Midwest Great Lakes region. Soon, a trio of influential leaders would lead a coalition that would change the Great Lakes landscape forever. Billy Caldwell, Shabbona, and Alexander Robinson would be given titles of "Chief". This title would replace the traditional Potawatomi village leaders' title and give the trio representation as tribal leaders in treaty negotiations.

The relentless advance of American settlement continued west, and Caldwell, Shabbona, and Robinson happened to be in the right place at the right time to negotiate one of the largest land deals in Midwest history.

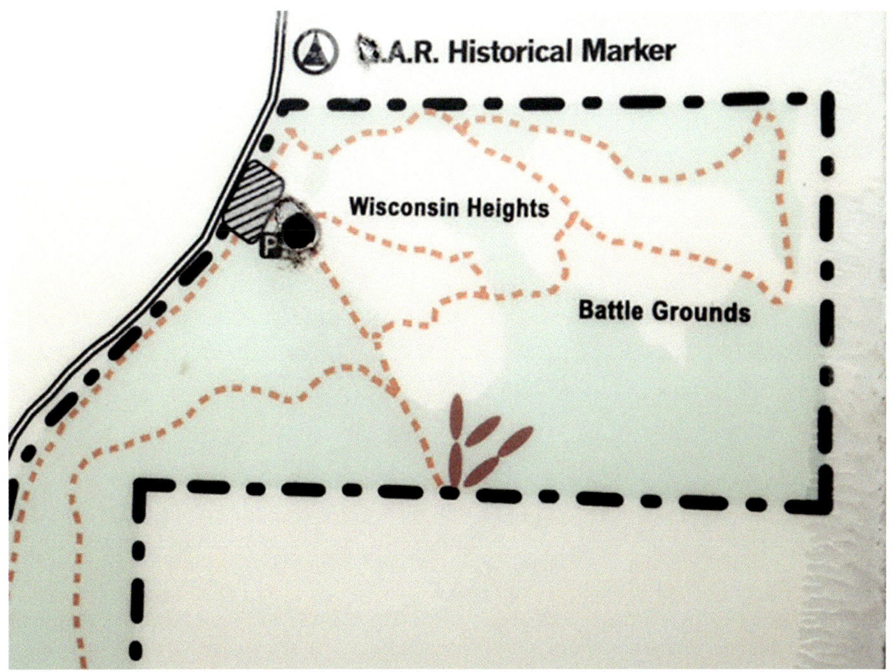

Wisconsin Heights' battlefield map. The Wisconsin Heights' battlefield is the only intact battle site from the Indian Wars in the U.S. Midwest. (*Image courtesy of Susan L. Kelsey*)

Wisconsin Heights' battlefield historic mounds. (*Image courtesy of Susan L. Kelsey*)

Sauganash Hotel. Important components of the new town were a post office, land office, newspaper, formation of a new county with Chicago the county seat, packing trade, lake harbor, schools, religious institutions, canal work, drawbridges, stage line to region, emigrant travel, pork packing, and land/lot speculation. (*Postcard courtesy of the Susan L. Kelsey private collection*)

Sauganash Hotel U.S. Stamp. By 1834, the mail route between Chicago and St. Louis was in operation. (*Stamp courtesy of the Susan L. Kelsey private collection*)

An 1833 Chicago map featuring a growing new city including Fort Dearborn (second fort built in 1816), Detroit Road, Green Bay Road, the first drawbridge located at Dearborn Street, a Catholic church, Temple Building, State Street, Dearborn Street, Clark Street, La Salle Street, Wells Street, Madison, Washington, Randolph and Lake Street, Sauganash Hotel and Tavern, Wolf Tavern, LaFramboise cabin and store, the first post office, and Billy Caldwell's home (left side of map). (*Image courtesy of the Chicago History Museum, ICHi-031183*)

6

1833: Moving West

It takes a thousand voices to tell a single story.

Tribe unknown

On the edge of the frontier, 1833 Chicago was home to a few hundred people, a fort, small buildings, and one way to cross the Chicago River. By September 26, 1833, the final treaty was signed, forever changing the course of the frontier town. Two years later, the treaty was ratified, and Billy Caldwell and 2,000 Native Americans left forever. Chicago, a strategic location for the U.S., was too important to not be a part of the new America. Sitting on the best port of Lake Michigan with links to the Des Plaines, Illinois, and Mississippi Rivers, Chicago would soon explode in population to more than 400,000 in forty short years to close to 3 million residents today.

Due to the 1833 Treaty, Illinois remains one of the few states without an in-state reservation. Today, the Chicago American Indian Center (A.I.C.) is the oldest, urban-based Native membership community center in the nation. The A.I.C. is the primary cultural and community resource for over 65,000 Native Americans in the greater Chicago metropolitan area and is home to the third largest urban population with more than 140 tribal nations represented. A new Native American Chamber of Commerce of Illinois today continues to advocate, educate and connect members in the Illinois area. Each year, the A.I.C. hosts its POW-WOW in Chicago and invites the public to learn more about Native American culture, food, and dance.

Back in 1833, Chicago was organizing itself as a new town. The State of Illinois had been admitted to the Union by 1818, Chicago was incorporated into a town by 1833, and the Potawatomi and allied tribes surrendered over 5 million acres of fertile land in northern Illinois and southern Wisconsin.

During 1827 and 1828, the Miller tavern was built by Samuel Miller on the north side of the intersecting river branches. It was used as a tavern, store, and home. In 1829,

A view of 1833 Chicago from "The Point." The view is looking north from the elevation at Franklin and Washington streets. Image includes the river ferry in the center of the image, cabins, and teepees located near each other, the Sauganash Hotel and Tavern, and prairie land outside of the fort boundary. (*Image courtesy of the Chicago Historical Museum, ICHi-005946*)

Display by the Chicago POW-WOW and hosted by the American Indian Center of Chicago. (*Image by Susan L. Kelsey collection courtesy of the Chicago POW-WOW hosted by the American Indian Center (A.I.C.) of Chicago*)

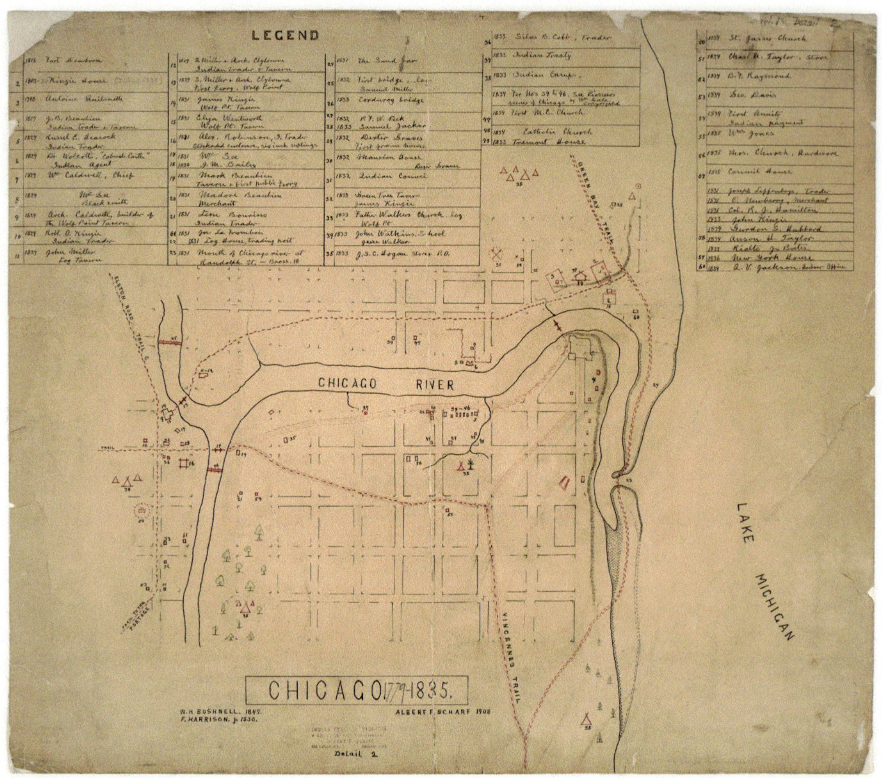

An 1835 map of Chicago featuring a grid-like street system, similar to present-day Chicago. (*Image courtesy of the Chicago History Museum, ICHi-068282*)

Elijah Wentworth occupied it. Also, at this location was a cabin used for a store by R. A. Kinzie and David Hall, later as Beaubien's Sauganash Hotel. A ferry was authorized for use by Archibald Clybourn and Samuel Miller near Wolf Point. They were taxed $2 and required to have a bond of $100.

Billy Caldwell's role in the 1833 Treaty was unique to the time and place in American history. His Mohawk heritage combined with experience in the British Army, fur trading, and emerging American roles placed him in a unique leadership position in 1833. A Métis with the advantage of knowing several languages and having the ability to move easily among Native Americans, the soldiers of Fort Dearborn, and Chicago pioneers, Caldwell was named "Chief"—a position of power—to negotiate the 1833 Treaty. As chief, Caldwell was the point person to represent the United Nations of the Chippewa, Ottawa, and Potawatomi.

The 1833 Treaty was between George B. Porter, Thomas J. V. Owen, and William Weatherford, commissioners of the United States on the one part and the United Nations of Chippewa, Ottowa, and Potawatamie Indians of the other part, being fully represented by the chiefs and head-men. The full text of the treaty is contained below:

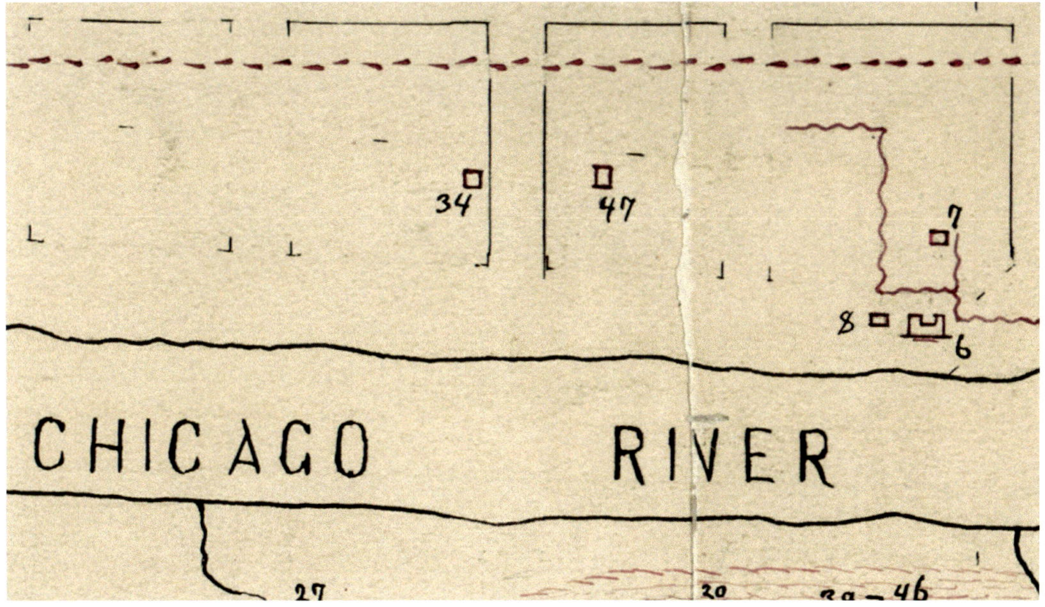

Above: An insert of the 1835 map includes the location of Caldwell's home, indicated by the number "7." This home was located north of the Chicago River around the present-day intersection of Chicago Avenue and State Street. The 1835 map includes structures, homes, and landmarks: Fort Dearborn, Kinzie house, Ouilmette house, Beaubien house, Alexander Robinson Indian trader, Bourassa Indian trader, LaFramboise Trading Post, Corduroy Bridge, and several churches. (*Image courtesy of the Chicago History Museum, ICHi-068282*)

Right: Caldwell, recognized as "Chief," and his home. (*Image courtesy of the Chicago History Museum, ICHi-068282*)

	1816	Fort Dearborn
2	1803-30	Kinzie House (Erected 1779)
3	1798	Antoine Ouilmette
	1817	J. B. Beaubien Indian Trader & Tavern
5	1827	Russel E. Heacock Indian Trader
6	1829	Dr. Wolcott, "Cobweb Castle" Indian Agent
7	1829	Wm Caldwell, Chief
8	1829	Mc Gee Blacksmith
9	1829	Arch. Caldwell, builder of the Wolf Point Tavern
10	1829	Robt. O. Kinzie Indian Trader
11	1829	John Miller Log Tavern

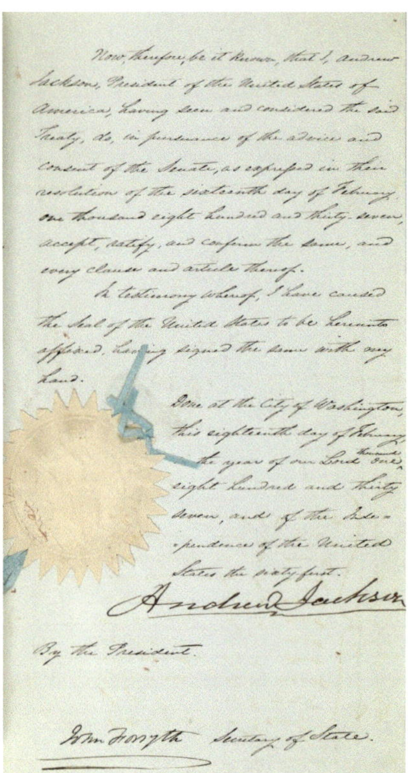

Now, therefore, be it known, that I, Andrew Jackson, President of the United States of America, having seen and considered the said Treaty, do, in pursuance of the advice and consent of the Senate, as expressed in their resolution of the sixteenth day of February one thousand eight hundred and thirty-seven, accept, ratify, and confirm the same, and every clause and article thereof.

In testimony whereof, I have caused the Seal of the United States to be hereunto affixed, having signed the same with my hand.

Done at the City of Washington, this eighteenth day of February in the year of our Lord one thousand eight hundred and thirty seven, and of the Independence of the United States the sixty-first.

Andrew Jackson

By the President.

Jno. Forsyth Secretary of State.

President Andrew Jackson signed the 1833 Treaty of Chicago. Signature is not the 1833 Treaty signature but represents the president's signature during that time period. (*Image courtesy of the U.S. National Archives, Treaties between Nations*)

ARTICLE 1st.The said United Nation of Chippewa, Ottowa, and Potawatamie Indians, cede to the United States all their land, along the western shore of Lake Michigan, and between this Lake and the land ceded to the United States by the Winnebago nation, at the treaty of Fort Armstrong made on the 15th September 1832 bounded on the north by the country lately ceded by the Menominees, and on the south by the country ceded at the treaty of Prairie du Chien made on the 29th July 1829 supposed to contain about five millions of acres.

ARTICLE 2d. In part consideration of the above cession it is hereby agreed, that the United States shall grant to the said United Nation of Indians to be held as other Indian lands are held which have lately been assigned to emigrating Indians, a tract of country west of the Mississippi river, to be assigned to them by the President of the United States to be not less in quantity than five millions of acres, and to be located as follows: beginning at the mouth of Boyer's river on the east side of the Missouri river, thence down the said river to the mouth of Naudoway river, thence due eat to the west line of the State of Missouri, thence along the said State line to the northwest corner of the State, thence east along the said State line to the point where it is intersected by the western boundary line of the Sacs and Foxes thence north along the said line of the Sacs and Foxes, so far as that when a straight line shall be run therefrom to the mouth of Boyer's river (the place of beginning) it shall include five millions of acres. And as it is the wish of the Government of the United States that the said nation of

Indians should remove to the country thus assigned to them as soon as conveniently can be done; and it is deemed advisable on the part of their Chiefs and Headmen that a deputation should visit the said country west of the Mississippi and thus be assured that full justice has been done, it is hereby stipulated that the United States will defray the expenses of such deputation, to consist of not more than fifty persons, to be accompanied by not more than five individuals to be nominated by themselves, and the whole to be under the general direction of such officer of the United States Government as has been or shall be designated for the purpose. And it is further agreed that as fast as the said Indians shall be prepared to emigrate, they shall be removed at the expense of the United States, and shall receive subsistence while upon the journey, and for one year after their arrival at their new homes. It being understood, that the said Indians are to remove from all that part of the land now ceded, which is within the State of Illinois, immediately on the ratification of this treaty, but to be permitted to retain possession of the country north of the boundary line of the said State, for the term of three years, without molestation or interruption and under the protection of the laws of the United States.

ARTICLE 3d. And in further consideration of the above cession, it is agreed, that there shall be paid by the United States the sums of money hereinafter mentioned: to wit.

One hundred thousand dollars to satisfy sundry individuals, in behalf of whom reservations were asked, which the Commissioners refused to grant: and also to indemnify the Chippewa tribe who are parties to this treaty for certain lands along the shore of Lake Michigan, to which they make claim, which have been ceded to the United States by the Menominee Indians the manner in which the same is to be paid is set forth in Schedule “A” hereunto annexed.

One hundred and fifty thousand dollars to satisfy the claims made against the said United Nation which they have here admitted to be justly due, and directed to be paid, according to Schedule “ B” hereunto annexed.

One hundred thousand dollars to be paid in goods and provisions, a part to be delivered on the signing of this treaty and the residue during the ensuing year.

Two hundred and eighty thousand dollars to be paid in annuities of fourteen thousand dollars a year, for twenty years.

One hundred and fifty thousand dollars to be applied to the erection of mills, farm houses, Indian houses and blacksmith shops, to agricultural improvements to the purchase of agricultural implements and stock, and for the support of such physicians, millers, farmers, blacksmiths and other mechanics, as the President of the United States shall think proper to appoint.

Seventy thousand dollars for purposes of education and the encouragement of the domestic arts, to be applied in such manner, as the President of the United States may direct.[The wish of the Indians being expressed to the Commissioners as follows: The united nation of Chippewa, Ottowa and Potawatamie Indians being desirous to create a perpetual fund for the purposes of education and the encouragement of the domestic arts, wish to invest the sum of seventy thousand dollars in some safe stock, the interest of which only is to be applied as may be necessary for the above purposes. They therefore request the President of the United States, to make such investment for the nation as he may think best. If however, at any time hereafter, the said nation shall have made such advancement in civilization and have become so enlightened as in the opinion of the President and Senate of the United States they shall be capable of managing so large a fund with safety they may withdraw the whole or any part of it.]

Four hundred dollars a year to be paid to Billy Caldwell, and three hundred dollars a year, to be paid to Alexander Robinson, for life, in addition to the annuities already granted them. Two hundred dollars a year to be paid to Joseph LaFramboise and two hundred dollars a year to be paid to Shabehnay, for life.

Two thousand dollars to be paid to Wau-pon-eh-see and his band, and fifteen hundred dollars to Awn-kote and his bands, as the consideration for nine sections of land, granted to them by the 3d Article of the Treaty of Prairie du Chien of the 29th of July 1829 which are hereby assigned and surrendered to the United States.

ARTICLE 4th. A just proportion of the annuity money, secured as well by former treaties as the present, shall be paid west of the Mississippi to such portion of the nation as shall have removed thither during the ensuing three years. After which time, the whole amount of the annuities shall be paid at their location west of the Mississippi.

ARTICLE 5th.[Stricken out.]

This treaty after the same shall have been ratified by the President and Senate of the United States, shall be binding on the contracting parties.

In testimony whereof, the said George B. Porter, Thomas J. V. Owen, and William Weatherford, and the undersigned chiefs and head men of the said nations of Indians, have hereunto set their hands at Chicago, the said day and year.

The 1833 treaty was ratified with a condition that the Native Americans leave within three years, which happened 1835 through 1837. Billy Caldwell, his children, Alexander Robinson, Joseph LaFramboise, and Beaubiens, and children of Ouilmette received cash *in lieu* of reservations.

Clifton, a Caldwell researcher, stated Caldwell's personality began to change at this point and he became a "protector" of Native Americans. The new role for Caldwell supported his decision-making process, first investigating living options in both Missouri and Iowa prior to the final move in 1834. Caldwell married his third wife, Saqua (Masaqua) LeGrand, a Métis of French and Potawatomi descent, on November 18, 1834.

For their part in the treaty, Caldwell Robinson and Shabbona received large tracts of land. Caldwell received 1,600 acres along the Chicago North Branch of the River in present-day Sauganash and Edgebrook neighborhoods on the north side of Chicago. Reportedly, Caldwell never lived on the land, but sold it before he left in 1835.

Caldwell's services were no longer needed or valued by the incoming Americans, so he chose to take annuities from the government and was employed as a Potawatomi chief. During this time, around 1834, his son, Alexander, died from the effects of alcohol and his daughter, Elizabeth, six years old, was very sick. Jesuits' notes recorded Elizabeth being baptized around this time. Billy Caldwell soon sold his 1,600 acres of land and headed west.

Today, a bronze marker located in the Sauganash neighborhood at the intersection of Kilbourne and Rogers commemorates the signing of the treaty and the boundary line between Fort Dearborn and Indian Country. The Edgebrook–Sauganash Historical Society is the steward of all thing's history in the North Chicago communities. Lawrence

444

TREATY WITH THE CHIPPEWAS, ETC. 1833.

In presence of Wm. Lee D. Ewing, Sec. to the Commission. E. A. Brush. Luther Rice, Intr. James Conner, Interpreter. Joseph Bertrand, Jnr. Interpreter. Geo. Kercheval, sub. Ind. agt. Geo. Bender, Major 5th regt. infy. D. Wilcox, Capt. 5th regt. J. M. Baxley, Capt. 5th Infy. R. A. Forsyth, U. S. A. L. T. Jamison, Lt. U. S. A. O. K. Smith, Lt. 5th Infy. J. L. Thompson, Lt. 5th inf. J. Allen, Lt. 5th inf. P. Maxwell, asst. surgeon U. S. A. Geo. F. Turner, asst. surg. U. S. Army. B. B. Kercheval. Thomas Forsyth. Daniel Jackson, of New York. J. E. Schwarz, Adjutn. Genl. M. M. Robt. A. Kinzie. G. S. Hubbard. L. M. Taylor. Pierre Menard, fils. Jacob Beeson. Samuel Humes Porter. Edmd. Roberts. Jno. H. Kinzie. Jas. W. Berry. Gabriel Godfroy, jr. Geo. Hunt. A. H. Arndt. Andw. Porter. Isaac Nash. Richard J. Hamilton.

To the Indian names are subjoined a mark and seal.

SCHEDULE "A,"

Referred to in the Article suplementary to the Treaty, containing the sums payable to Individuals, in lieu of Reservations of Land.

		Dollars.
Po-ka-gon		2000
Rebecca Burnett	Edward Brooks Trustee for each	500
Mary Burnett		250
Martha Burnett (R. A. Forsyth Trustee)		250
Madaline Bertrand		200
Joseph Bertrand Junr		200
Luke Bertrand Junr		200
Benjamin Bertrand		200
Lawrence Bertrand		200
Theresa Bertrand		200
Amable Bertrand		200
Julianne Bertrand		200
Joseph H. Bertrand		100
Mary M. Bertrand		100
M. L. Bertrand		100
John B. Du Charme		200
Elizabeth Du Charme (R. A. Forsyth Trustee.)		800
George Henderson		400
Mary Nado and children		400
John Bt. Chandonai		1000
Charles Chandonai	For each of whom R. A. Forsyth is Trustee	400
Mary Chandonai		400
Mary St. Comb and children		300
Sa-gen-nais' daughter		200
Me-chain, daughter of Pe-che-co		200
Alexis Rolan		200
Polly Neighbush		200
Francois Page's wife and children		200
Pierre F. Navarre's children		100
Jarmont (half breed)		100
Ten thousand dollars		$10,000

Sept. 27, 1833. Agreeably to the stipulations contained in the Articles supplementary to the Treaty, there have been purchased and delivered at the request of the Indians, Goods, Provisions and Horses to the amount of fifteen thousand dollars (leaving the balance to be supplied hereafter ten thousand dollars.)

Schedule "A" on the 1833 Treaty of Chicago indicating the sums paid to individuals *in lieu* of land or reservations. (*Image courtesy of the United States National Archives*)

Signature of Billy Caldwell on national treaty. (*Image courtesy of the United States National Archives*)

Plaque located in present-day Sauganash neighborhood at the intersection of Kilbourne and Rogers, Chicago. The plaque reads: "OLD TREATY ELM." The tree that stood here until 1933 marked the northern boundary of the Fort Dearborn reservation, the trail to Lake Geneva, the center of Billy Caldwell (Chief Sauganash) reservation and the site of the Indian Treaty of 1833. Erected by Chicago's Charter Jubilee Authenticated by Chicago Historical Society 1937. (*Image courtesy of Susan L. Kelsey*)

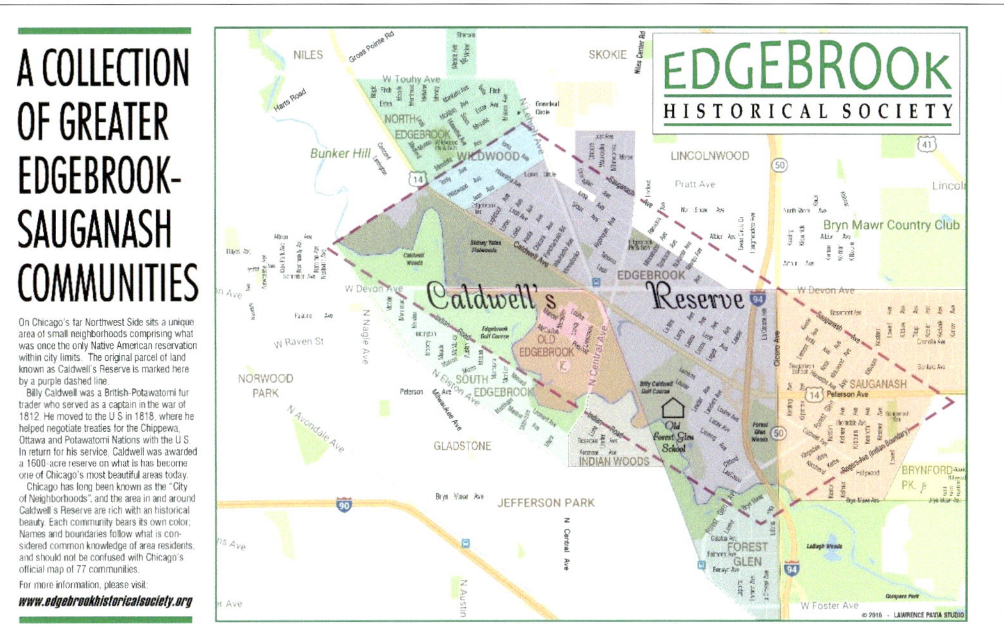

Map by Lawrence Pavia, Edgebrook Historical Society of present-day Edgebrook and Sauganash neighborhoods, with an overlay of the location of the Caldwell 1,600-acre reserve. Today, Caldwell Avenue bisects the historic reservation and is a diagonal street connecting the two Chicago neighborhoods. The north branch of the Chicago River runs along the south side of the Caldwell reserve. (*Image courtesy of Lawrence Pavia private collection*)

Pavia, creator of the Caldwell Reserve drawing, demonstrates the vastness of the reserve had Caldwell stayed in the area.

An old boundary line runs through Sauganash, the Chicago neighborhood, located on the north end of the Chicago city limits. Sauganash is home to the 39th Ward, a strong Catholic community, and Queen of All Saints Basilica. Queen of All Saints Church displays a stained-glass window detailing the Sauganash story and signing of the treaty. A branch of the Chicago River runs along the south end of the Sauganash neighborhood and cuts through the Billy Caldwell Golf Course and Edgebrook. The river runs through Bunker Hill Woods Preserve and Indian Road Woods Preserve. A little further west lies the property of Billy Caldwell's friend, Alexander Robinson, with easy access to the Des Plaines River. Alexander Robinson lived on the Chicago reserve with his family until his death in 1872. The last of the chiefs, Shabbona received land and a fresh spring 70 miles west of Chicago. Named Shabbona's Grove, Shabbona and 130 members moved to their new location.

Chief Shabbona (also spelled Chamblee, Chab-o-neh, Shabonee, and Shab-eh-nay) was born around 1775 around the Ohio River area and was the son of Ottawa Tribe. Like many other tribes, his family moved west to the Illinois area late 1700s. The land was stolen from Shabbona, and today, Shabbona's Grove is a state park and lake.

Shabbona's Grove located in DeKalb County was nestled in a grove of trees in a beautiful small valley. Shabbona Lake State Park is located at the site and the landscape

Old tonic advertising label featuring Chief Shabbona and tonic ad from Ottawa, Illinois. (*Image courtesy of the Susan L. Kelsey private collection*)

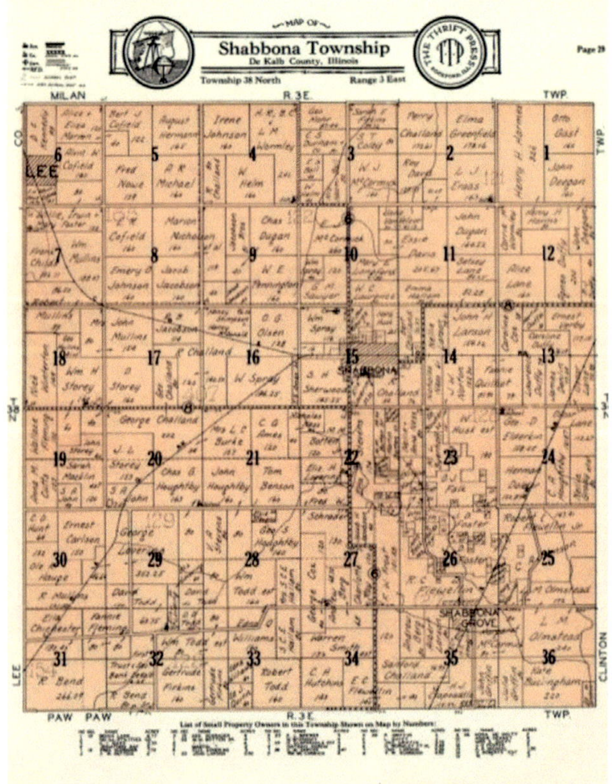

Thrift Press. Atlas and plat book of De Kalb County, Illinois: compiled from surveys and the public records of De Kalb County, Illinois. (*Image courtesy of the Library of Congress, Rockford, Ill.: Thrift Press, 1929. Map. www.loc.gov/item/2007626890*)

Entrance sign to the Chief Shabbona Forest Preserve located in DeKalb County. Historic trails led visitors past bent trail marker trees and old growth woods. (*Image courtesy of Susan L. Kelsey*)

has changed due to a reservoir. The original Indian Creek that ran through Shabbona's Grove was dammed up and now a lake is used for recreation.

Shabbona was a large man with a wide face. An Ottawa Native whom allied with the Chippewa and Potawatomi in a United Nations called "The Three Fires." Jean Baptiste Beaubien's first wife was Mah-naw-bun-noquah, an Ottawa Indian, sister of Chief Shabbona. He was the grandnephew of the great Indian Chief Pontiac. In the 1829 treaty, Shabbona received two sections for a home for Shabbona and his family. This tract of land included Section 23, and the west half of Section 25, and the east half of Section 26, east of the Third Principal Meridian at Paw Paw Grove.

The tract of land included 1,280 acres of most beautiful grove of trees and protected valley. When Caldwell's band left in 1835, most of Shabbona's family was required to leave. From 1835 until 1849, he often visited them and Caldwell until 1841. Unfortunately, during his travels, nearby settlers cut his timber and eventually stole his land. When Shabbona returned, he was not allowed to live there so he lived on a 20-acre tract, south of Morris, donated by patriotic white people until he died in 1859.

Settlers' stories describe a familiar sight of Shabbona riding his pony across Illinois to visit his friends. He would have been around seventy-five years of age. He would ride the trails and the settlers would look for him every spring and fall to make sure he was still alive. His wife, Coconako (or Pokanoka), weighed over 400 pounds and

Historic Shabbona Grove, home to Chief Shabbona's clan and granted in the Treaty of 1829. Indian Creek provided fresh spring water to Shabbona's family and tribe. (*Image courtesy of Susan L. Kelsey*)

Grave marker of Chief Shabbona and his family, located in Evergreen Cemetery, Morris, Illinois. (*Image courtesy of Susan L. Kelsey*)

traveled sitting in the box of a wagon. She died on November 30, 1864 when her wagon overturned crossing the Mazon Creek. The grandchild trapped underneath her died as well. Shabbona died on July 17, 1859, near Morris Falls, Illinois, aged eighty-four years—this was eighteen years after Billy Caldwell died. He and his wife were buried in Morris in Evergreen Cemetery. His cemetery monument was dedicated on Friday, October 23, 1903.

The time had come for the Potawatomi and allied tribes to leave Chicago. On June 6, 1835, over 2,500 Native Americans left Chicago under Captain J. B. F. Russell, government agent. On September 9, Capt. Russell placed a notice in one of the local papers:

> WANTED FOR THE REMOVAL OF INDIANS.
> From 10 to 40 Ox Teams. The waggons to be strong and well made, with good canvass or cotton covers, to keep everything within dry-to carry with it a bucket for tar or greese-to be supplied with an axe, or hatchet, hammer, and nail.s. Each waggon to have two yoke of Oxen, to carry 1500 lbs. if required, and to travel daily twenty miles, if necessary. A per diem allowance will be paid, commencing on the day the team is accepted, which will include all allowances, except to the teamsters, a pound of bread and meat will be issued and forage to the Oxen. This allowance to continue until the arrival of the party at the country allotted to the Indians west, and a day's pay for each twenty miles for their return to Chicago. The United States will not be responsible for any accident that may accrue.-The teamsters are implicitly to obey all reasonable orders and directions from any government agents. No teamster under 18 years of age will be accepted. It is reserved to the government agent in charge of the party, to discharge a team at any time by allowing him his return pay as above stipulated. Proposals to be made to the subscriber, at his office, in Col. John H. Kinzie's store, on or before the 19th of September.
> J. B. F. Russell,
> Capt. U.S. Army, Military Disb'g Agent.
> Chicago, Sept. 9, 1835. 140

According to the State of Illinois Museum documents, Christian B. Dodson, who had come to Chicago in August 1833, received the contract to furnish transportation for the Potawatomi, and the wagon train left Chicago on September 21 for the rendezvous point on the Des Plaines River, 12 miles from Chicago. Four groups, under the leadership of Alexander Robinson, Billy Caldwell, Waubonsee, and William Holiday, left the Des Plaines River on September 28 and were assisted by Robert Kinzie and Kercheval. The train proceeded west to Skunk River.

In Caton's *The Last of the Illinois and a sketch of the Potawatomis* (1870), a great war dance was performed in front of the parlor windows of the Sauganash Hotel. The hotel was located at present-day north side of the Chicago River.

Warriors streamed past the hotel, faces painted with war symbols, tomahawks waving in the air, whoops and hollering in a mad war dance. Caton, a witness of the event, stated: "What if they should in the madden frenzy, turn this sham warfare into a real attack? How easy it would be for them to massacre us all and leave not a living soul to tell the story."

Chief Shabbona grave marker in Evergreen Cemetery, Morris, Illinois. (*Image courtesy of Find-a-grave website*)

Map of the trail of Billy Caldwell starting at Fort Niagara, New York, through Michigan, Illinois, to his final resting place, Council Bluffs, Iowa. (*Image courtesy of the Susan L. Kelsey private collection*)

Image of Sauganash Hotel, owned by Mark Beaubien and named after Billy Caldwell, Chief Sauganash. (*Postcard courtesy of the Susan L. Kelsey private collection*)

The Potawatomi tribe started from the banks of Fort Dearborn, present-day at Michigan Avenue and Wacker Drive, proceeded down the south side of the Chicago River, which would be present-day Archer Avenue. They continued for 8 miles until they reached the confluence of the Chicago River and the Des Plaines River. At this point, they met with Chiefs Shabbona and Robinson for a final farewell. Over 2,000 Indians had joined the Chief for the journey to their new home. They headed southwest, followed an old Indian Trail, leftover from the Ice Age, and marched out of town, never to look back.

7

1837: The Trail of Politics

What is life? It is the flash of a firefly in the night. It is the breath of a buffalo in the wintertime. It is the little shadow which runs across the grass and loses itself in the sunset.

Blackfoot

Caldwell led his tribe of over 2,000 members over the Mississippi River at the modern-day Oquawka (pronounced, oh-KWAW-kuh) "yellow banks" village. Oquawka was a military fort on the Mississippi in the early 1800s, providing access over a narrow section of the river. From Oquawka, Caldwell led his tribe through Mount Pleasant, Iowa, and then headed south to St. Joseph, Missouri. During this time period, the Sioux Indians were located in northern Iowa and the Caldwell tribe moved along the southern end to avoid conflict.

The crossing at Oquawka would have been all about the logistics: food, camping, and transportation. This crossing location was well-known among the Native Americans and early explorers because of the narrow geography at the Mississippi. An early historical marker is located at present-day Oquawka, indicating the location of an old trader's log cabin from 1827.

Caldwell's tribe arrived in either the St. Joseph, Missouri, or St. Louis, Missouri, area in the fall of 1835. Both towns are located on the Missouri River, former French trading posts, and early 1800s military posts. Indian Agents were individuals authorized by the new U.S. government to interact with Native American tribes. Indian agencies were located throughout the new United States and used Indian Agents to deal with Indian tribes, negotiate treaties, prevent conflicts between settlers and Indians, distribute federal annuities, and oversee removal of Indians from new settlements. Agency, Missouri, is located between St. Louis and St. Joseph and may have been a resource for Caldwell and his group. Agency records at the Missouri location include visits by

A 300-year-old oak witness tree on the eastern edge of the Mississippi River in the town of Oquawka. Picture on the right is an old road running along the edge of the river, used for the port and transportation. This was the crossing location during the removal of Caldwell Potawatomi's. (*Image courtesy of Susan L. Kelsey*)

Above left: Today, the Port of Oquawka is home to around a thousand locals that use the port for recreation. (*Image courtesy of Susan L. Kelsey*)

Above right: A mural image from the Oquawka Park displays the ferry use in earlier times. (*Image courtesy of Susan L. Kelsey*)

Joseph Robidoux (1783–1868), a fur trader. Robidoux, also spelled various ways, knew Caldwell in Michigan and Illinois during the peak fur trading days.

Billy and his tribe arrived in Platte County, Missouri, and were dependent on Fort Leavenworth (Kansas) for food and supplies. They stayed in the area for eighteen months before leaving for Iowa. Platte County was excluded from the state of Missouri in 1820 but later included due to its 2 million rich and fertile acres. Six counties were added, resulting in a final Missouri state status.

Earlier in 1803, Robidoux tried to set up fur trading operations at Fort Dearborn but was defeated by the Forsyth–Kinzie partnership. He moved his fur-trading operation to St. Joseph with special permission from the federal government. Robidoux and Caldwell had years of history together, and some references say Robidoux was at Caldwell's side during his death to record his last will and testament. Robidoux is considered the founder of St. Joseph, Missouri. The St. Joseph–St. Louis area was positioned to take advantage of the emerging new westward trails and pioneers moving across America. The pony express began later in St. Joseph around 1860.

As with many early towns, St. Joseph began as a fur-trading post. French-Canadian Joseph Robidoux III located his Blacksnake Hills post at the entrance to the Indian-controlled Platte country so he could trade cloth, metal pots, and other manufactured goods for Native Americans' furs. According to the book *Old Saint Jo, Gateway to the West, 1799–1932* by Sheridan A. Logan, Robidoux actually knew Billy Caldwell in 1804 when Robidoux visited Fort Dearborn. Robidoux tried to sell furs in

Welcome to St. Joseph, Missouri, sign. Explored by the French in the 1700s, used by fur trader Joseph Robidoux at the turn of the nineteenth century, St. Joseph was officially founded in 1843. (*Image courtesy of Susan L. Kelsey*)

St. Joseph, Missouri around the mid-1800s. St. Joseph is home of the Pony Express National Museum. Although the Pony Express did not officially begin until April 3, 1860, the museum has a lot of history about the area, including the Platte Purchase. (*Photo by Susan L. Kelsey, courtesy of the St. Joseph Pony Express Museum*)

the Chicago area, but was forced to leave and set-up shop south in St. Joseph. Later, when Billy Caldwell moved to Council Bluffs, he was still friends with Robidoux, and Robidoux managed his money during when Caldwell was away on hunting trips.

Concurrently, the Louisiana Purchase, although completed in 1803, excluded a triangle section of northern Missouri, the location of St. Joseph and Buchanan County, Missouri, and Billy Caldwell's camp. The entire county was excluded from the original treaty of Prairie du Chien when ceded the land to the Sac, Fox, and Ioway Indians in 1830. In 1837, the Platte Purchase added Buchanan County and 2 million additional acres of land to the state of Missouri.

The land was fertile, hilly, and bustling with commerce—a dramatic difference compared to the north Council Bluffs, Iowa, location where Caldwell and his band would be relocating in eighteen short months.

Although Billy Caldwell led a delegation to Missouri in 1834 to inspect their newly assigned reservation, negotiations were already in the process to procure the Platte Purchase. As a result of Platte Purchase of 1836, Caldwell and his band were removed from Missouri north to Iowa territory at Traders Point. Dissatisfied with what they

The Platte Purchase, painted by George Gray, depicts the signing of the Platte Purchase Treaty between the Iowa and Sac and Fox Tribes, and the United States Government in 1836. The Treaty added the Platte Territory to the State of Missouri. Counties carved from the Platte Territory are Atchison, Nodaway, Holt, Andrew, Buchanan and Platte. Lewis Fields Linn was the U.S. Senator responsible for getting the treaty ratified by Congress in 1837. (*Photo by Susan L. Kelsey, courtesy of the St. Joseph Pony Express Museum*)

found, Billy sought a large territory in northern Illinois but was unsuccessful. The choice of Council Bluffs was the last option.

Caldwell and his tribe of 500 people remained in the northwest corner of Missouri until their final destination to Council Bluffs, Iowa. During that stay, he camped on property located a few miles east of Fort Leavenworth.

Prior to the Louisiana Purchase, Missouri excluded a triangle of land in the northwest section of the state. This land was the home of several tribes: the Sac, Fox, Sioux, Omaha, Iowa, and Oto. It was here that Father Charles Felix Van Quickenborne, on January 29, 1837, baptized fourteen Indian children in the Potawatomi camp opposite Fort Leavenworth. The first of the number baptized, Susanne, the six-month-old daughter of Claude LaFramboise and a Potawatomi woman, had William, or as he was familiarly known in Chicago, "Billy" Caldwell, for godfather, who also stood sponsor for two more of the children. Other sponsors on this occasion were Claude LaFramboise, Toussaint Chevalier, Joseph Chevalier, Francis Bourbonnet, and Michael Arcoit. Father Van Quickenborne was in fact dealing with a group of ex-residents of Chicago or its vicinity, some of whose names had appeared on the poll-book of the election of 1826, the first in the history of the city.

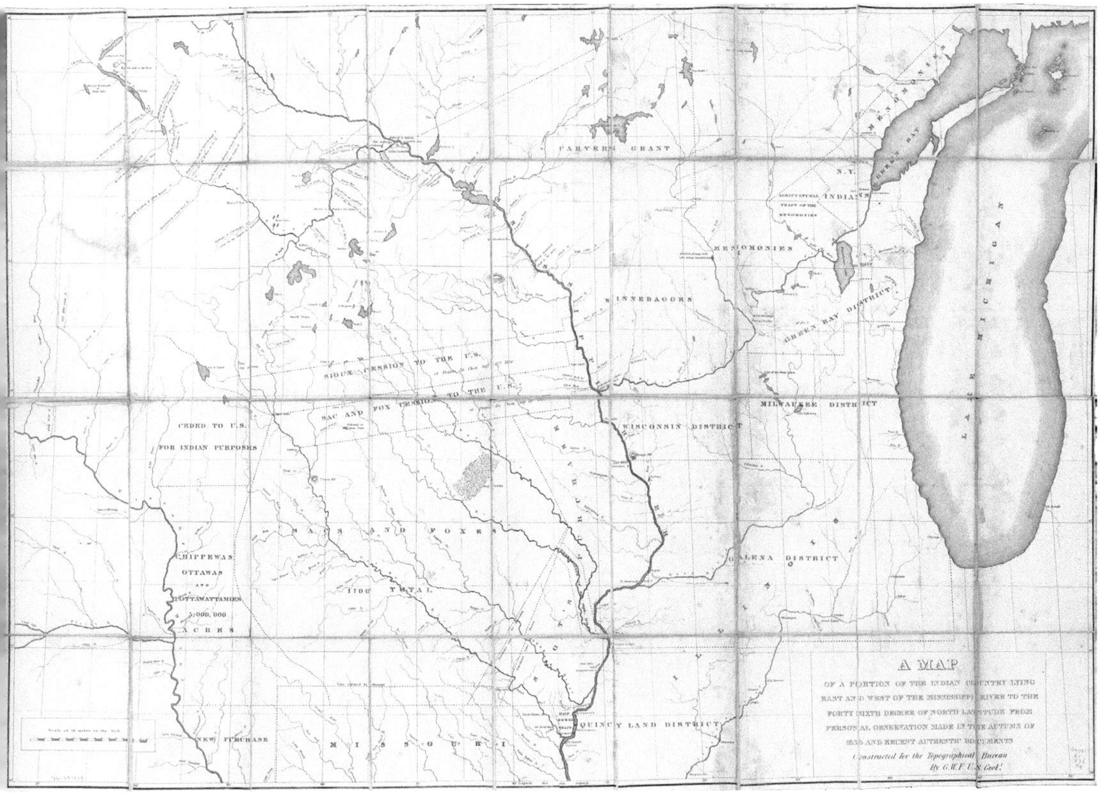

Above: A map of a portion of the Indian country lying east and west of the Mississippi River to the 46th degree of north latitude from personal observation made in the autumn of 1835 and recent authentic documents. Produced by George William Featherstonhaugh and United States Topographical Bureau. (*Image courtesy of the Library of Congress, www.loc.gov/item/96683128)*

Right: Historic Fort Leavenworth sign on the edge of the prairie. (*Image courtesy of Susan L Kelsey*)

According to the *Annals of Platte County*, there are three areas that Native Americans were stationed outside of Fort Leavenworth. One area was opposite from Fort Leavenworth, across the river on the Missouri side near present-day Weston. This is near the lost town of Rialto just to the south, on the bluffs, now part of the Weston Bend State Park. At one time, the military issued rations from the park land, but the location is now closed.

The second possible location was called Potawatomi Prairie, located a few miles west of Platte City, east of Fort Leavenworth, and a third location was located at the Indian Agency, called Agency Ford on the Platte River, now present-day Agency, Missouri.

In the *Annals of Platte County* (1839), Billy Caldwell received his rations from the fort at an issue house also known as a general resort area. The Native Americans were rationed beef, bacon, and flour. In the *Annals*, the issue house was located and built 60 yards north of the Whitely property, located near present-day Beverly Station, located 2 miles east of Fort Leavenworth. It lies at the junction of Highway 92 and 45. It was east enough to be far from the flooding Missouri, flat for camping, and close to water sources. Bee Creek runs through the area and would have provided transportation access to the Missouri as well as food and recreation.

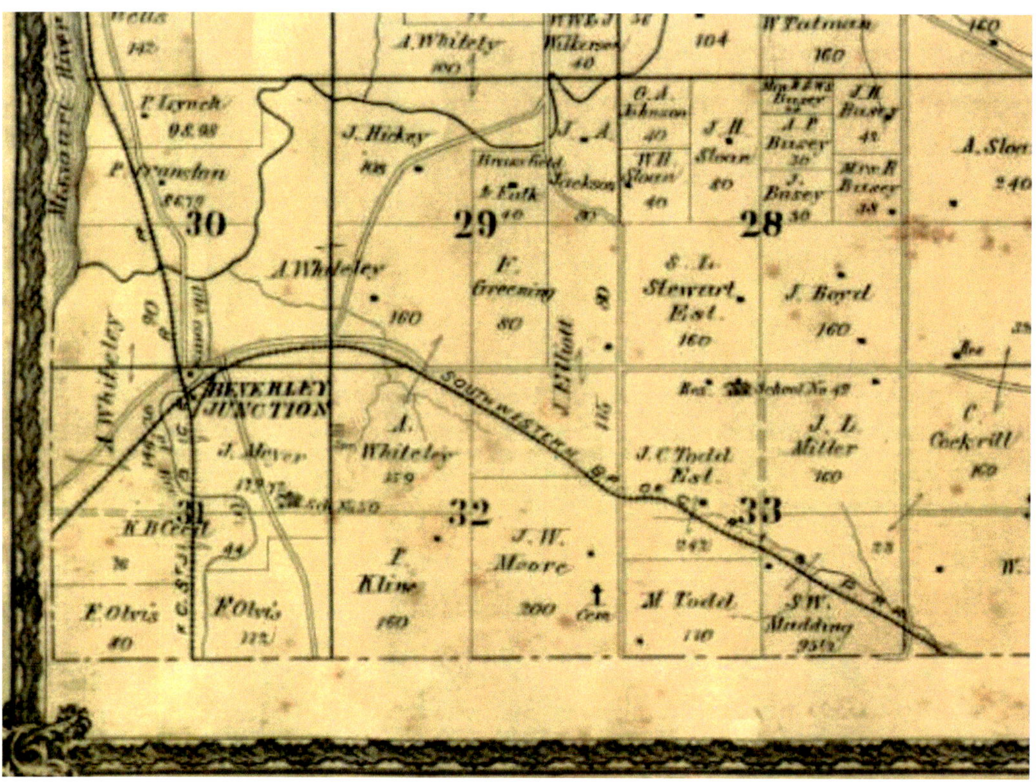

Beverly Station, located on the left side of the map is located in Missouri, east of the Missouri River and Fort Leavenworth. The map was a major intersection of commerce during the early 1800s. Bee Creek runs north and south on the map and provided fresh drinking water. On the middle of the map, toward the bottom, note the Todd Family plat with a cemetery cross just to the left of the Todd plat. (*Image courtesy of the Annals of Platte County, Missouri*)

An historic trading post at the Beverly Station, Missouri. The building is located just east of Fort Leavenworth. (*Image courtesy of Susan L. Kelsey*)

Based on the three possible campsite locations, it was determined that the Caldwell camp was located on private property. The campsite was located on a property owned by the Todd Family and an article in the *Missouri Annals of History* provided additional information about the character of Billy Caldwell, Chief Sauganash. The Caldwell campsite was discovered based on the location of the historic Todd family cemetery, Hackberry Road, Beverly Junction, Missouri. The *Annals* provided testimony that a gentleman by the name of Joseph Todd owned property three 3 miles west of the falls in Platte City and on the military road. This area was called Todd's Settlement and was located about 4 miles east of Fort Leavenworth and about 2 miles east of present-day Beverly. In Todd's notes, he referred to Billy Caldwell as Socanois or "Sauganash."

Todd's testimony provided a direct reference to the location of Billy Caldwell's campsite outside of Fort Leavenworth. An old map with a family cemetery cross provided the location on the Todd property.

Among a rolling hillside and sweeping farm homestead is the Todd family cemetery. Joseph Todd (died April 29, 1876 at the age of sixty-eight years and two months) and the owner of the homestead was buried in the family plot. Caldwell would have camped on the Todd property, often called Todd's Settlement.

PERSONAL NOTES—JOS. TODD (iii).

Mr. Todd having been driven from the claim he selected in 1835 on Todd's Creek, which took its name from him, he applied for permission to settle on the Military Road, three miles west of the Falls. This license was granted him, and the rich body of hackberry lands is still called the Todd Settlement. His neighbors were Martin, at the Falls, and Boulware, Brown, and Williams, at the Issue House. The Pottawatomies were around him, and the old chief, called Col. Caldwell by the whites, and known by his warriors as Socanois, pitched his wigwam in Mr. Todd's yard. He took pleasure in reciting his adventures in broken English. He claimed that he was with Tecumseh at the battle of the Thames. With assumed dignity, he would say: "Before the battle, Tecumseh gave me the order: 'You go to the left, and I will go to the right. But farewell; you will never see me again.'" Socanois was straight, and about 6 feet 3 inches high. He was kind and genial, and a great favorite with Mr. Todd's family. He had some education, and read newspapers with difficulty. He was much interested in the Florida War, and did not conceal his sympathy for the Indians. Mr. Todd's post-office was at the Fort,

Old news article with personal notes from Mr. Todd regarding Billy Caldwell. (*Image courtesy of the Annals of Platte County Missouri*)

Map insert of Todd Family plat and family cemetery where Caldwell and his band camped while in Platte County, Missouri. (*Image courtesy of the Annuals of Platte County Missouri*)

Above: Todd's Settlement and family gravesite, located on Hackberry Road, near Beverly Junction, Missouri. (*Image courtesy of Susan L. Kelsey*)

Right: Homesteader Joseph Todd's gravestone. (*Image courtesy of Susan L. Kelsey*)

By February 1837, the Senator Linn Treaty was ratified by Congress, and the following July, Caldwell left Platte County for good and moved north 150 miles to Council Bluffs, Iowa.

With the newly created state of Missouri, Caldwell and his band were forced to move north, 150 miles to Council Bluffs, Iowa. Over 2,000 people migrated north with Caldwell. The sick and elderly took a steamboat. Ottawa and Ojibwa also were with the band, but all were identified at Potawatomi. The band left on July 1837 and travelled for over twenty-three days until they reached the Council Bluffs blockhouse, located high up on the hill in Council Bluffs, Iowa, present day at the intersection of Union and Pierce Roads. Today, apartment buildings replace the old blockhouse, but Iowa Historical Society plaques designate the corners of the old blockhouse.

On July 28, 1837, Caldwell and his 2,000-member tribe began the final move north to Iowa. On July 28, Brigadier General H. Atkinson, commanding the First Department of the Western Division of the Army, and Dr. Edwin James, Indian Sub-Agent in charge of the Pottawattamies, accompanied seventy-five to 100 women, children, and sick Indians on a steamer called *Kansas* and took them north up the Missouri River to present-day Council Bluffs. Caldwell's village encompassed no more than 500 members with the rest of the other chiefs creating another five villages in the surrounding area:

> Sir:—
> Having been ordered by the General in Chief of the Army, bearing date 20th June, and given in conformity with instructions from the Secretary of War of the 19th of June to remove the Pottawattamie's to their lands agreeably to the treaty made on the 26th September, 1833, and ratified 21st February, 1835, and having landed a portion of them at this point, and the residue being on their march and will shortly arrive, I consider the object of the Government accomplished...
>
> With respect, Sir, Your Ob't Serv't
> H. Atkinson, Brig. Gen'l.
>
> Dr. Edwin James,
> Sub-Agent for Pottawattomies.

Captain Moore also marched with the tribe. It took twenty-three days by land to march from Fort Leavenworth to Council Bluffs. Along the way, two to three members of Caldwell's tribe died. On August 5, the steamer *Kansas* arrived. By November 11, the blockhouse was finished, and General Moore returned to Fort Leavenworth. In all, the Chicago Natives numbered around 1,200 people, with another 1,300 removed from the Great Lakes areas, totaling around 2,500 of Native Americans moving to western Iowa on the Missouri River. Caldwell's band numbered around 500 Native Americans, the remainder of the Pottawatomies (Big Foot, Waubaunsee,) located in four to five other villages on the western front of Iowa. Caldwell led his band to Council Bluffs, Iowa, to start a new beginning.

This is an original painting by Geo. Catlin of St. Louis in 1832 showing a side paddle wheel steamer named the *St. Louis* headed up the Mississippi River under steam, with a view of the Saint Louis waterfront in the background. This steamboat would be similar to the steamboat used to move the Caldwell band north to Iowa on the Missouri River. (*Image courtesy of the Library of Congress. www.loc.gov/item/2014647409*)

8

1838: A New Beginning

Man has responsibility, not power.

Tuscarora

Council Bluffs, Iowa, located on the east bank of the Missouri River and east of Omaha, Nebraska, is in the county seat of Pottawattamie County, Pottawatomie County, named after first nations. (Spelled differently than the Native American spelling).

Thirty-three years before Caldwell arrived, Meriwether Lewis and Captain William Clark led an expedition to the Pacific Northwest in 1804.

A "council" was held with the members of the Otoe tribe and the area became known as "Council Bluff." The Missouri River, flowing the entire length of the state of Iowa, is the longest river in the United States, beginning in the western Rockies of Montana, flowing south, and entering the Mississippi River around St. Louis, Missouri. The river was a natural boundary line between a growing new America and western Indian country.

Geographically, the city boasts of a unique feature called the Iowa Loess Hills. The Loess Hills run north–south 200 miles along the Missouri River, a leftover from the retreat of the Wisconsin Glacier 14,000 years ago. The Loess Hills stand out as a unique defining character of the divide between Iowa and Nebraska and stands 200 feet higher than the prairie land to the west. One can only imagine the thought of pioneers heading across the prairie in covered wagons, seeing the rise of the Loess Hills and then nothing but prairie, flat across Nebraska as far as the eye could see. The hills are made of gritty, yellowish sediment known as loess. It is a wind-deposited silt, often near river-valley sources. The loess sediment is a constantly changing and fragile landscape in Council Bluffs and erosion of the bluffs is a perennial challenge. In fact, the loess material is a substantial character in the death and burying ground of Billy Caldwell as narrated in future chapters.

Above: A map showing the Pottawattamie Indian land in 1835, present-day Council Bluffs. Chippewa, Ottawa, and Pottawattomi land included 5 million acres along the Missouri River and Mosquito Creek. The map also included a triangle section of the Missouri that Caldwell and his band lived at for eighteen months before moving north to present-day Iowa. Featherstonhaugh, G. W. & United States Topographical Bureau (1836). A map of a portion of the Indian country lying east and west of the Mississippi River to the 46th degree of north latitude from personal observation made in the autumn. (*Courtesy of Library of Congress, www.loc.gov/item/96683128/. Library of Congress, Geography and Map Division*)

Below: A map of Lewis and Clark's track, across the western portion of North America from the Mississippi to the Pacific Ocean: by order of the executive of the United States in 1804, 1805, and 1806. The map includes Council Bluffs, Iowa, Mosquito River, and the Platte River intersecting the Missouri River.(*Image courtesy of the Library of Congress, www.loc.gov/item/79692907*)

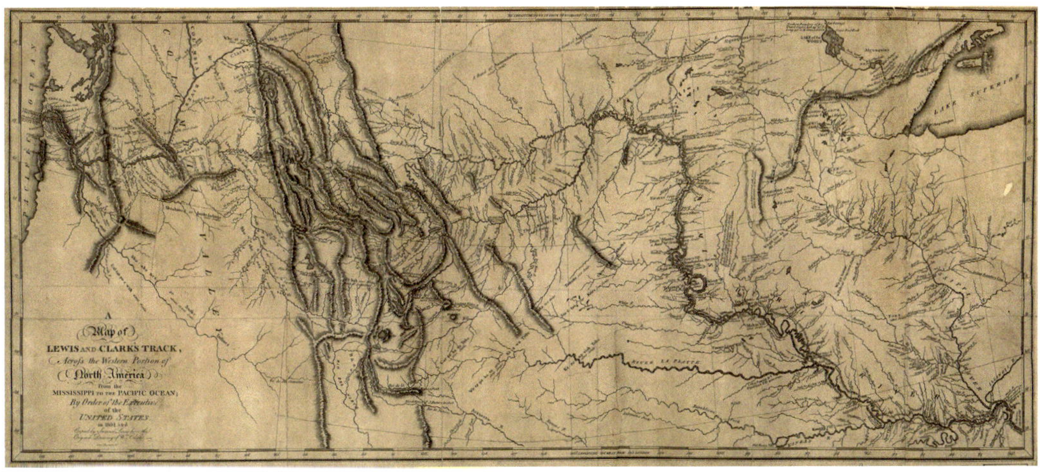

Map insert showing location of Council Bluffs, Mosquito Creek, Nishnabotoma River, and the Missouri River.

A view of the Loess Hills in Council Bluffs, Iowa, from the Omaha, Nebraska, airport tarmac, looking east. (*Image courtesy of Susan L. Kelsey*)

Bellevue Log Cabin, located in Nebraska, west of the Missouri River. Built in 1835 originally down by the flood plains, the cabin was moved to the upper plateau in 1850. (*Image courtesy of Susan L. Kelsey*)

Across the Missouri River on the Nebraska side, another trader had set up operation by the name of Peter A. Sarpy. Caldwell and Sarpy would have known each other and work together during the 1830s. Today, you can visit an historic trader's cabin in Nebraska. It was moved from the edge of the Missouri River and relocated in Nebraska and continually used until the 1970s.

Prior to Billy Caldwell and his tribe arriving in Council Bluffs, the area was a significant trading post. In 1834, John Jacob Astor retired from the American Fur Company and it was bought by Pratte, Chouteau and Company. As early as 1824, Peter Sarpy (at the age of nineteen) worked for the American Fur Company's trading post. They traded often with local Indian tribes: the Siouan-speaking Omaha, Ponca, Otoe, and Pawnee. The fur trade in the region yielded such profits that for decades it was the most important driver of the St. Louis economy. In 1821, it represented $600,000 of the town's annual commerce of $2 million. Sarpy later established a trading post and supply point for white settlers and pioneers on the Iowa side of the upper Missouri River. It went by various names, including Sarpy's Point and the "Trader's Post."

Indian agencies were established south near St. Louis and eventually over twenty-five forts or blockhouses were built along the Missouri River in the early 1800s. Fort Leavenworth is south of Council Bluffs and a sub-agency was built in current-day Bellevue, Iowa, located around 15 miles south of the present-day Council Bluffs. It became known as the Council Bluffs agency in 1833.

Bellevue Log Cabin, a pioneer residence in 1835, it was used throughout the years as a residence and restored in 1972 and entered on the National Register of Historic Places. (*Image courtesy of Susan L. Kelsey*)

Bellevue, Mr. Dougherty's agency on the Missouri. The illustration shows buildings, paddocks, settlers, ox cart, and Indians at Bellevue, Major John Dougherty's trading post on the Missouri River. (*Image courtesy of Bodmer, Karl, Artist. Bellevue. Mr. Dougherty's agency on the Missouri / Ch. Bodmer pinx ad nat; L. Weber & Beyer sc. [Between 1832 and 1843] Photograph. Retrieved from the Library of Congress, www.loc.gov/item/2007683615/*)

Feeding into the Missouri River are several tributaries, Boyers Creek, Welch's Creek, Mosquito Creek Five Barrel Creek, and Nishnabotna Creek. The Caldwell Potawatomi camp was located on the bluff at present-day Council Bluffs, Iowa. Some 10 miles south, labeled Hamilton's Trading House, was the French trading post also called Trader's Point or Point aux Poules.

The most reliable source of information regarding the Potawatomi in this area is in the book *Early Days at Council Bluffs* by Charles H. Babbitt. After writing for the Nonpareil newspaper for several years, he moved to Washington, D.C., where he had access to the files at the Department of Indian Affairs, the War Department, etc., and could find the truth among the several versions he had heard about the history of the city.

In fact, the county was named Pottawattomie County, Iowa, because of the Billy Caldwell tribe, although the spelling is different.

The U.S. government built a military blockhouse high up on the Loess Hill, east of the Missouri River in present-day Council Bluffs. Upon arrival at the new home in Council Bluffs, Iowa, the Caldwell band found a military blockhouse about 200 feet above the Missouri River.

The Council Buffs blockhouse was built sometime between August and November 1837 by the U.S. Dragoons and under instructions from Col. Kearney of Fort

OLD BLOCKHOUSE (SUPPOSITITIOUS PICTURE)

An 1837 Council Bluffs, Iowa, blockhouse. This picture probably completed by Captain D. B. Moore in 1837. No portholes are shown because the U.S. did not use cannons to control. The building was a simple hewn-log structure, 24 feet square, without openings on the north and west sides except loopholes for small-arms fire. After it came into the possession of the Jesuit missionaries, small windows were cut in the building. (*Image courtesy of Pottawattamie County IAGenWeb*)

Leavenworth. It stood for about twenty years until 1857. Captain D. B. Moore was commissioned to provide protection to the incoming Potawatomi Indians from the northern Sioux tribes and as an issue house for government supplies. The blockhouse was located at present-day East Pierce Street between Grace and Union Streets. It was the nucleus around which the City of Council Bluffs was later built. It was built of simple, hewn-logs, 24 feet square, without openings, later windows were cut open. O. J. Pruitt, historian and author, described the blockhouse as a simple structure, with no further need by the military.

On September 1, 1837, Davis Hardin was appointed assistant Indian farmer. He arrived to assist Billy Caldwell and his tribe to farm the Iowa land and was charged with assisting the new community in ways of farming the land. He later stayed there with his family and cemetery headstone is locate in Fairview Cemetery.

According to research, around 2,000 Indians left for Council Bluffs. It appears that they separated into four communities: one at Trader's Point (LaFramboise), a second at the Blockhouse (Caldwell), a third at Iranistan near the East Nishnabotna River located near present-day Iowa State University (Bigfoot), and the fourth was located near Tabor, Iowa (Wabaunsee, also spelled Waubansie). The Iowa State Park named for him is spelled Waubonsie. Big Foot's village to be located about 50 miles northeast of Council Bluffs, on Indian Creek, a tributary of the Nishnabotna River. Caldwell's village had around 500 members. The 2,000 total Native Americans had split up into four

Gravesite of Hardin family, former Indian agent to Caldwell. Located in Fairview Cemetery, Council Bluffs, Iowa. (*Image courtesy of Susan L. Kelsey*)

communities. Another community was set up by Chief Johnny Green in nearby Tama and Marshall Counties.

Hardin and his family and a company of soldiers arrived on the *Antelope* steamer from Fort Leavenworth. This would have been a significant event since up until this time, the area was only frequented by fur trappers and traders. Now, around 2,000–3,000 Indians had arrived in the area escorted by the U.S. military. What a sight this must have been. They camped on a natural spring at the bluff that eventually became Council Bluffs. The spring has long since been either rerouted or covered up by streets.

On September 12, 1837, a petition letter signed by Billy Caldwell, Waubaunsee, Le Clair, and others requested a mission and school be built in Council Bluffs. Father Verhaegen and the Missouri Senator Benton visited the White House in Washington, D.C., and met with President Van Buren. The petition was granted, and in response to this request, Father Pierre-Jean De Smet and Father Verhaegen received passports to travel to Indian Territory (present-day Council Bluffs) to start their mission.

The blockhouse was given to the Caldwell band and camp was set up around the structure. Caldwell only remained here three years before his death in 1841. The rest of the band was moved to new reservations in Kansas just five years later by 1846.

Catholic missionaries Father DeSmet and Father Verhaegen arrived in Council Bluffs, Iowa, on May 31, 1838. According to the *Life, Letters and Travels of Father Pierre-Jean de Smet, S.J., 1801–1873*, it was written:

> Four poor little cabins besides made of rough logs, fourteen feet each way with a roof of rude rafters, which protect us neither rain nor hail, and still less from snow in winter. Don't protect against rain, hail, less from snow in winter. We arrived among the Potawatomi's on the afternoon of the 31st of May. Nearly 2,000 savages, in their finest rigs and carefully painted in all sorts of patterns, were awaiting the boat at the landing. I had not seen so imposing a sight nor such fine-looking Indians in America.

However, Babbitt stated the Natives were not necessarily waiting for the missionary, but rather the shipment of supplies on the boat. In 1839, the chapel was enlarged, and a new house was built by missionaries.

During the course of DeSmet's ministry, 308 baptisms were performed. The first recorded was Elizabeth Catherine Bourbonne on June 9, 1838 and the last recorded baptism was July 17, 1841. For marriages, the first entry was August 15, 1838 between Pierre Chevalier and Louis Ouilmette. In all, De Smet performed twenty-two marriages, with the last one dated January 5, 1840. De Smet left Council Bluffs later that spring of 1840. The last marriage performed in Council Bluffs was by Father Christian Hoecken on January 28, 1841.

The *Illinois Catholic Historical Review* (Vol. 1, No. 2, pages 164 and 165) records of the mission state, on August 15, 1838, Father Peter DeSmet, the noted Indian missionary, performed two marriage ceremonies at Council Bluffs, the first recorded in the history of the place. The contracting parties were Pierre Chevalier and Kwiwatenokwe, and Louis Wilmot (Ouilmette) and Marie Wa-wiet-mo-kwe. On January 2, 1839, the same priest married William Caldwell to Susanna Misnakwe. (The document also mentions that he was godfather to several children.) Clifton writes that his fourth wife was identified as a French woman named Susanne Misnawke.

Site of Council Bluffs Blockhouse located at present-day intersection of Pierce and Union streets. Former map shows Potawatomie Camp, Bellevue (Trader's Point) and the creeks and rivers leading to the Missouri River. (*Babbitt image courtesy of personal collection of Mary Lou McGinn*)

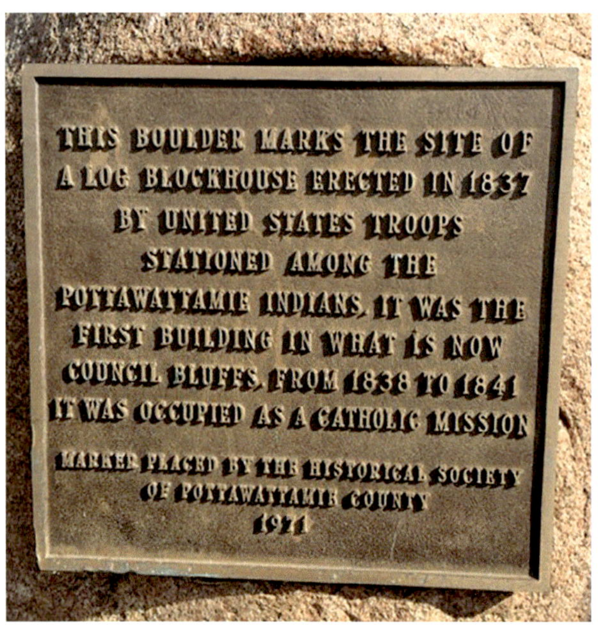

Located on the west corner of the former blockhouse, the brass plaque inscription states, "This boulder marks the site of a log blockhouse erected in 1837 by United States Troops stationed among the Pottawattamie Indians, it was the first building in what is now Council Bluffs, from 1838-1844 it was occupied as a Catholic Mission." Marker placed by the Historical Society of Pottawattamie County, 1874. (*Image courtesy of Susan L. Kelsey*)

This plaque, located on the east corner of the former blockhouse, is inscribed with the following statement, "Pierre Jean De Smet, S.J. Peacemaker, Jesuit Missionary. Ministered to the Pottawattamie Indians 1838–1840 in the Blockhouse built near this spot by U.S. Dragoons in 1837, with love, faith and courage he labored for the cause of humanity." Marker place by the Historical Society of Pottawattamie County, 1971. (*Image courtesy of Susan L. Kelsey*)

The Council Bluffs blockhouse, later transformed into the St. Joseph's Mission, sketched and interpreted by George Simon in 1855. (*Image courtesy of Annals of Iowa, Babbitt, 1896*)

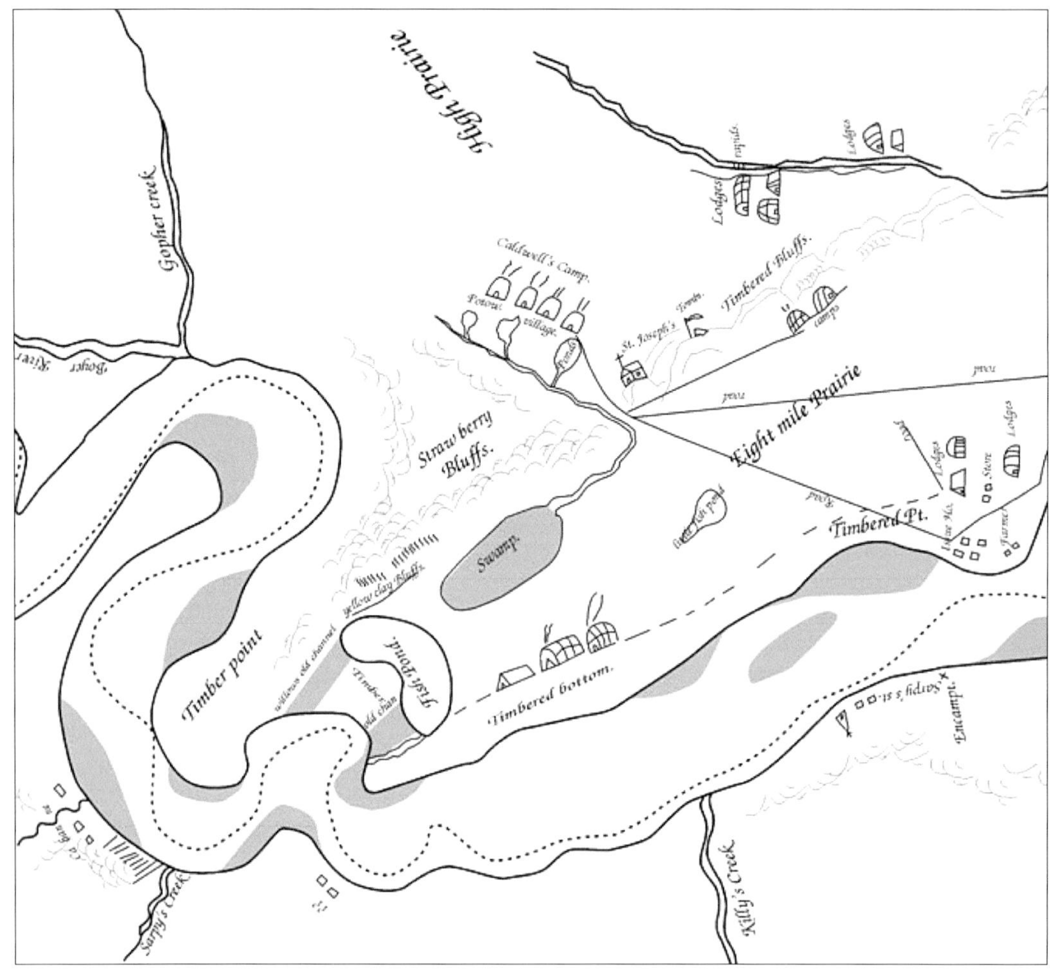

A remarkable 1839 Council Bluffs map by Father DeSmet. (*Image courtesy of Council Bluffs Public Library, accessed April 14, 2019, www.councilbluffslibrary.org/archive/items/show/2624*)

William E. Whittaker, Office of the State Archaeologist with the University of Iowa, wrote a wonderful article, "Pierre-Jean De Smet's Remarkable Map of the Missouri River Valley, 1839: What did he see in Iowa?" Using De Smet's map, William compared the georeferenced digital land copies of the 1852 General Land Office township maps. Bill writes: "The locations of steep bluffs, and the locations of major streams emerging from the bluffs, were fairly easy to determine based on comparisons between De Smet's map and the modern USGS maps."

One creek that was problematic was Mosquito Creek because the meandering path over the years. De Smet wrote of Council Buffs: "It was common to meet bears in the neighborhood, wolves would come to the doors and they had to be continually on guard against the Sioux." They always walked around with a good knife or tomahawk. He would often take canoe trips down the Missouri River and witness the sandbars and swift flowing river that gave it its character.

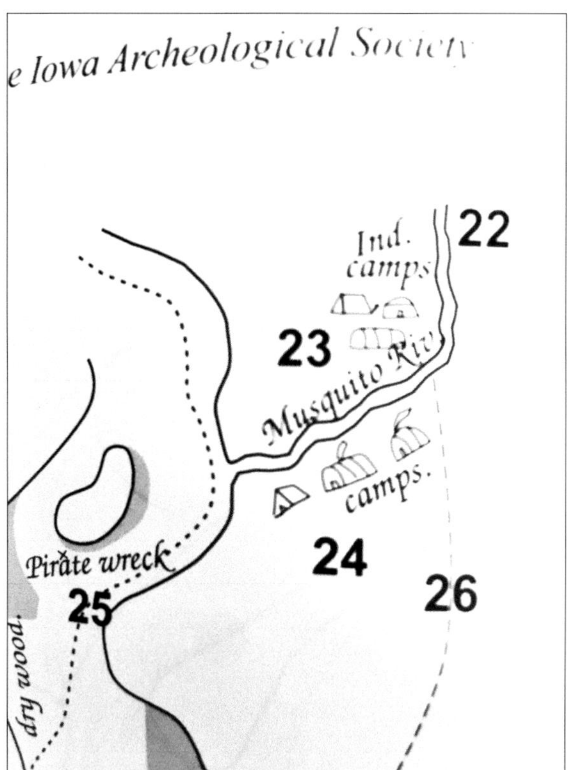

Archeologist William Whittaker compared the De Smet map to present-day landmarks. Number 22 represented Mosquito Creek, a meandering creek that has shifted its course over time. Number 23 and 24, represented an area of Indian Camps. Number 25 represented the shipwreck of the Steamboat Pirate. *(Image courtesy of William Whittaker, University of Iowa)*

Number 25 representing the shipwreck of the Steamboat *Pirate*. According to Whittaker, the *Pirate* was loaded with much-needed supplies and sank in the Missouri just short of its destination in April 1839:

> _____ Nicollet witnessed the *Pirate's* sinking and described the event, "At about 5:00 we passed by the wreck of the steamboat. We can only see the top of the roof and the portholes of the state cabins. A few Indians, prowling around the wreckage to pull a few pieces off it, cast a shadow of sadness over our thoughts."

The *St. Louis Daily Missouri Republican* published a summary of the wreck on May 6, 1839.

> Steamboat *Pirate* Lost—
> From the Captain of the Wilmington we learn that the steamer *Pirate*, about seven miles below Bellview (Bellevue) and about 26 miles below Council Bluffs on her passage up the Missouri, was snagged sunk and is considered a total loss. She was freighted with flour, bacon, corn, & etc. intended for the Pottawatamie and Otoe Indians. The freight was received at Liberty. It is also probable that she may have had on board a portion of the Fur Companies goods designed for the Indian trade. She was insured in this city for about $12,000. Her cargo, it is probable, was insured here but to what extent

is at present unknown. A hand from the *Pirate* who came down on the Wilmington represents her as being sunk in very deep water that it is thought no attempt will be made to raise her.

In the spring of 1839, food was scare and there was a threat of a Sioux attack. The sinking of the *Pirate* was untimely and desperate times for the Caldwell band. Soon after by the fall, De Smet left the mission. The winter of 1840 was one of the harshest one on record.

Trader's Point was located 14 miles south of Council Bluffs along the Missouri River on the Iowa side. Originally a fur-trading post in the 1820s, Points aux Poules was a bustling trading center with several homes and families working in the area. An Indian agency was later established for the Otoes, Pawnees, and Omahas at Bellevue and became known as the agency of Council Bluffs. It was a favorite site for Caldwell to hang with fur traders and exploders travelling up and down the Missouri River.

Trader's Point, also known as Point aux Poules, was one of several fur-trading locations along the Missouri River. Fur traders were usually Métis, mixed blood of French and Native American descent. Furs were repacked at Point aux Poules and sent south to the market in St. Louis.

Today, the site is located near the flood prone Missouri River. Currently, a log cabin built by Benjamin Marks in 1905 occupies the area. Some of the first American wagon trains going to California crossed the Missouri River nearby the trading point.

Local Council Bluffs historian, Mary Lou McGinn states Caldwell died at Trader's Point and was carried back to the blockhouse where he was buried behind the military structure.

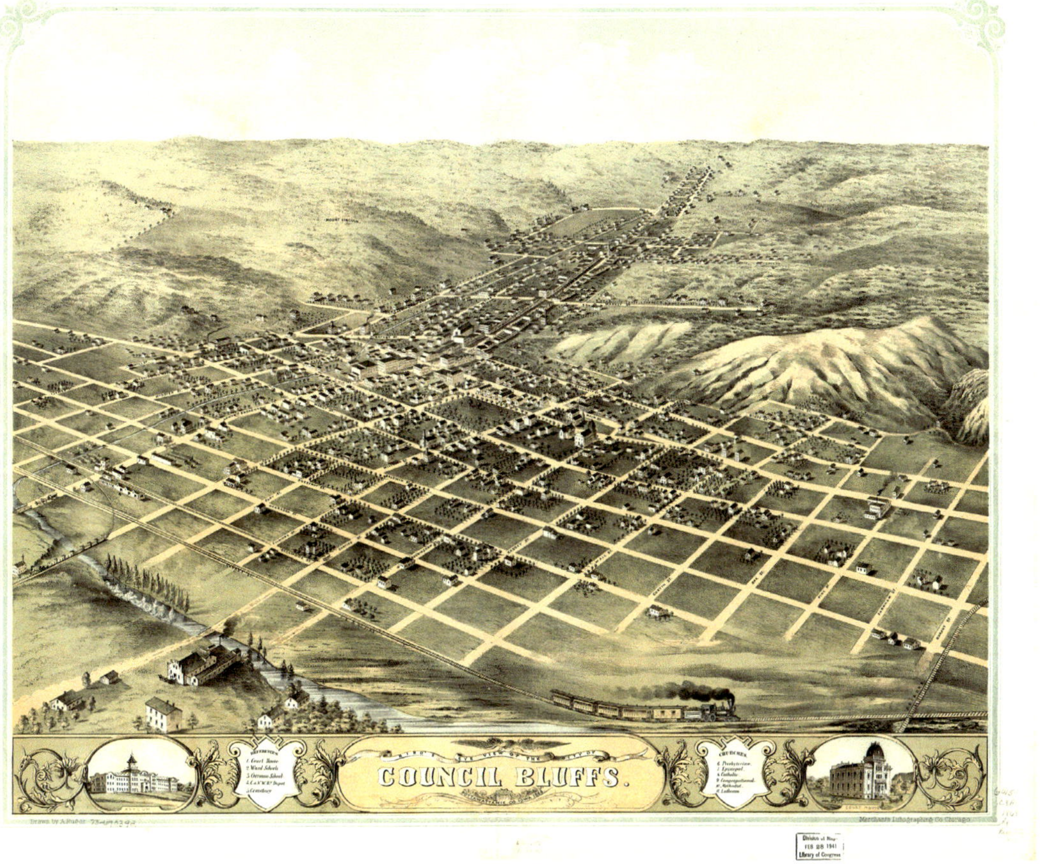

Above: Council Bluffs, nestled in the valley of the Loess Hills. (*Image courtesy of the Library of Congress, Ruger, A, and Merchant's Lithographing Company. Bird's eye view of the city of Council Bluffs, Pottawattamie Co., Iowa. [Chicago, Merchants Lithographing Co, 1868] Map. www.loc.gov/item/73693392*)

Right: Traders Point, also known at Point aux Poules, is located 10 miles south of the City of Council Bluffs. Caldwell had his office at Trader's Point. (*Image courtesy of Babbitt, Early Days at Council Bluffs, 1907*)

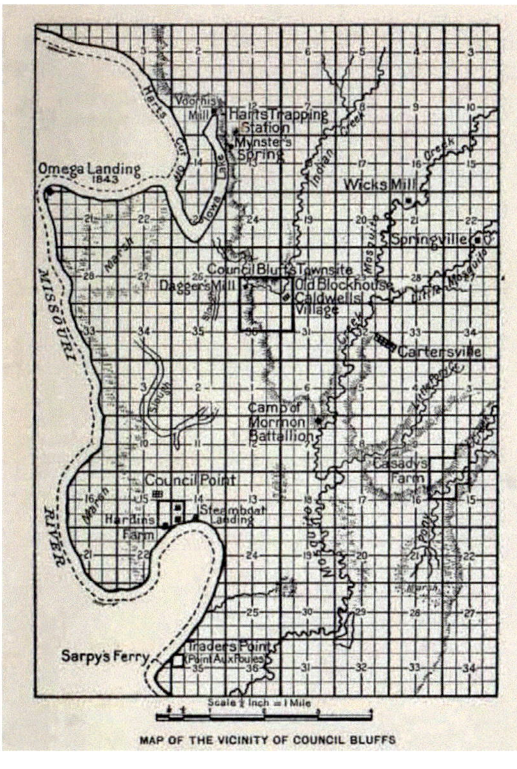

Left: Point aux Poules, located south of Council Bluffs about 10 miles was the site of French fur trading post and village. (*Image courtesy of Susan L. Kelsey*)

Below: Point aux Poules, present-day log cabin. (*Image courtesy of Susan L. Kelsey*)

9

1840: Native Entrepreneurship

A single twig breaks, but the bundle of twigs is strong.

Tecumseh

By 1840, Council Bluffs and other towns along the Missouri River were the gateway to the pioneering great west. In the eastern United States, strategic canals were already built, linking oceans, rivers, and lakes through canals like the Erie Canal and the newly created I&M canal. With the disappearing fur trade industry, new commerce enterprises were taking hold and expanding across the country. Use of new connecting waterways, trails, and westward migration created more opportunities for commercial enterprises along the Missouri River.

Commerce radiating out from Chicago, now connected through the I&M Canal and linking to the Illinois river and feeding into the Mississippi River, allowed new settlers to migrate north and south in the country. The Missouri River connected at St. Louis and provided a westward connection to the Rockies and eventually the Pacific Ocean.

In Council Bluffs, Caldwell and his band were at one of the gateways of the soon to be Oregon Trail. The geography, as a result of the glacier, provided rivers, streams, and creeks a runoff into the Missouri River. West of the Missouri River, flat prairie land was as far as the eye could see to the Rocky Mountains. The Oregon Trail, launched from St. Joseph, Missouri, was an opportunity for Caldwell and his band to be entrepreneurs and create a source of income for the reserve. To leverage their natural resources, Caldwell built a saw and grist mill on Mosquito Creek, about 3 miles northeast of the blockhouse and near present-day Highway 120 and Highway 6. Mosquito Creek flowed south to the Missouri River, a busy, trader's commerce route.

In 1840, Caldwell and his band requested funds from the U.S. government, but they were never received before Caldwell died in 1841. Caldwell and the other chiefs built

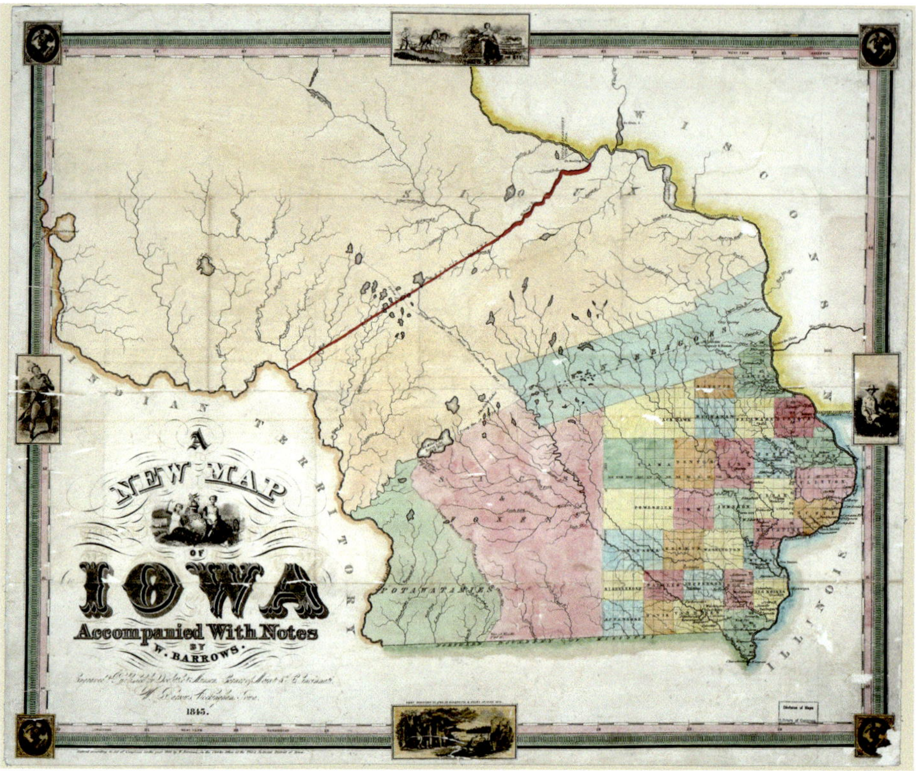

Above: Barrows, Willard, and Doolittle & Munson. A new map of Iowa: accompanied with notes by W. Barrows. Cincinnati: Engraved & published by Doolittle & Munson, 1845. (*Map courtesy of the Library of Congress, www.loc.gov/item/2007626856/. www.loc.gov/item/2007626856*)

Left: View of the Missouri River facing south with the City of Omaha pictured on the left and Council Bluffs on the right. (*Image courtesy of Susan L. Kelsey*)

Council Bluffs was one of the gateways to the Oregon Trail. With the ability to receive resources from the Missouri River, Council Bluffs was poised to launch travelers leaving on the Oregon Trail. (*Image from the collection of Susan L. Kelsey*)

Potawatomi mill built by Caldwell, LaFramboise and others at the cost of $3,000. The mill was located at the intersection of Hwy 120 and Highway 6, Council Bluffs, Iowa. (*Image courtesy of Babbitt, Early Days at Council Bluffs, 1907*)

the mill at a cost of $3,000, pledging their personal credit and annuities in payment. Caldwell's mill was part of a larger economic community with four local village leaders including Billy Caldwell, Joseph Laframboise, Bigfoot, and Waubaunsee. Each of the leaders, having come west from Chicago to settle in Iowa, created a western Iowa community of Indian Chiefs. Laframboise and his band maintained residency near Trader's Point. Bigfoot's clan was located about 50 miles east of Caldwell's village near Indian Creek and Nishnabotna. Wabaunsee's village was south of the present-day Tabor area. So, the location of the mill was convenient to the region's economic needs and access to transportation. The mill was used to grind grain and saw lumber.

The mill was ready for use in early 1841. It had a 40-foot dam crossing Mosquito Creek, with timbers 8–9 feet tall. The timbers created a crib that trapped the creek flow and rerouted it through the mill. The cribs were filled with earth to prevent the wash out of the mill foundation. The mill had both a saw and grist mill. The saw was used on local timber and the grist mill used two grinding stones, about thirty inches in diameter, to remove the bran from corn. The mill was not used for manufacturing fine flour, according to Babbitt. The strategic location on Mosquito Creek gave the mill enough torque and power to turn the water wheel, about 10 feet in diameter. The mill was known as the "Pottawattamie Mill" while operated by the Indians.

Up until 1840, Caldwell had been receiving annuities from the 1833 treaty in the amount of around $1,000 per year. However, he was concerned that they w ould be ending, so in 1841, he and Joseph LaFramboise build the first saw and grist mill using their own money. They requested the funds from the government, but never received them.

Following the death of Caldwell, the mill was run by several different families with names documented by the Council Bluffs Indian Agency—Holcomb, Parks, and Wicks. The payment and reimbursement of the mill came into question with the death of Caldwell. For the next four years, the chiefs tried to secure reimbursement.

The following documentation is important because it demonstrates the daily difficulty the Caldwell band had in trying to provide for their families, it documents family names that will become the founders of present-day Potawatomi Nations, it provides details about the mill, and, finally, it documents the fact that Caldwell and his band paid for the mill and were prepared to live an independent life.

> On February 21, 1842, from the files of the Council Bluffs Indian Agency letters, Roll 215.... To our Great Father, the President of U. States: We the undersigned chiefs of the United Nation of Ottawa's Chippewa & Pottawattamie respectfully represent that we have had built for our use a saw & grist mill which have cost us three thousand dollars & we respectfully ask that the 3d Article of the treaty concluded with us on the 23d September 1833, ratified 21 Feb. 1835 may be so far complied with as to give us the means to pay the workman for said mill & take it into possession. Signed on February 21, 1842 by the Council Bluffs Sub Agency and the names of Shab-oh-nay (his mark), Wau-bon-seh (his mark), Pad-a-go-shuck (his mark), Joseph La Fromboise (his mark), and Wobsi (his mark).

Map of mill location, Council Bluffs, Iowa. (*Image courtesy of Mary Lou McGinn*)

An 1840 Potawatomi mill located on Mosquito Creek, Council Bluffs. (*Image courtesy of Babbitt Early Days at Council Bluffs, 1916*)

Old waterwheel gristmill creating commerce for the Potawatomi Band in Council Bluffs, Iowa. (*Image courtesy of Babbitt Early Days at Council Bluffs, 1916*)

Example of grinding stone used to grind corn and wheat for animal feed. The mill was powered by a water wheel located on the river. This example of a millstone is from Vincent's Grist Mill formally located in Lincolnshire, Illinois. (*Image courtesy of Susan L. Kelsey*)

Letters from the Council Bluffs Indian Agency included: On February 23, 1842, a letter stated: "A mill has been built here. Caldwell [*sic.*] and LaFramboise contracted for its building. The machinery and dam are good. Mills [*sic.*] work well. They are still in possession of the contractor, who operates them." Later on April 5, 1842, a letter stated: "C. B. Indians Sub-Agency have built both a saw and grist mill, both in full operation. Aren't paid for," which was signed by Deaderick, sub-agent. The following year, on March 28, 1843, a letter stated: "C. B. Sub-Agency: $3000 paid to Samuel R. Holecomb for building grist and saw mill by contract dated Sept. 4, 1840, between Holecomb and B. Caldwell and other chiefs." In June 1843, letters stated: "Mills of the Indians in tolerable order, and blacksmith shop is being erected at the mills, having flooding forcing removal from the river." The following year, a letter was sent from the Council Bluffs Indian Agency, August 15, 1849. "Dear Sirs: I have just seen an article in the Frontier Guardian respecting the Pottawatamie Mill. The mill stones have been paid for by the Indians and receipts are on file in the sub-agents office of the above Indians." On July 30, 1853, the National Archives Indian Records Case No. 138 documents: "Pottawattomie Mill Reserve Near Kanesville, Iowa. The mill is on Musketoe Creek. The mill house is a small frame building about 20 x 25 feet, two stories high and a very indifferent one. The machinery, dam and under works are old and inferior (1853). It has one run of stones and a small trifling bolt, and is worth about $2,000 including water right and a mill yard."

The mill was the initiative of Shab-on-nay, Wau-bon-seh, Pad-a-go-shuck, Joseph LaFramboise, and Billy Caldwell. They were the men who in 1840 had contracted with Samuel R. Holcomb. Today, one can observe the old mill foundation located on Mosquito Creek. Overgrown and barely noticeable with a modern freight train bridge located over the top of the mill foundation, stone foundation rocks are covered by 200-year-old trees and weeds.

The mill location was found using the map and old Scofield family cemetery plat. The mill was located east of present-day Council Bluffs, located on the northeast corner of Highway 6 and 120. The mill foundation shares clue of its past. As noted above, the mill location was used by other operators, taking advantage of the quick bend at the creek.

Timbers from a long-lost sluice bed that crossed the creek remain in the cold creek, but their original builder will forever be a secret. Grist mills ground grain into ground meal or flour for use in bread. Caldwell's mill was water-powered with a long sluice gate that allowed water to flow under a water wheel, making it turn. A large gear turned a millstone that ground the flour. The mill was located near trails and waterways, making it easy to get products to and from the mill.

The mill provided the political autonomy that Caldwell craved and the economic security to replace the long-forgotten U.S. government annuities. Located near one of the launching points of the Oregon Trail, Caldwell's entrepreneurship had been a new source of income for his band.

Above: Location of the old Potawatomi mill on Mosquito Creek, Council Bluffs, Iowa. (*Image courtesy of Susan L. Kelsey*)

Left: Mill foundation covered with 200-year-old oak tree. Remnants of the old foundation, timbers, and cut stones still at the edge of the creek. (*Image courtesy of Susan L. Kelsey*)

Right: Hand cut stone foundation covered by 200-year-old oak tree. (*Image courtesy of Susan L. Kelsey*)

Below: The mill was used to create commerce and to take advantage of the geography of the land, creating a sustainable income for the Caldwell band. (*Image courtesy of Susan L. Kelsey*)

10

The Legacy of Billy Caldwell

Sing your death song and die like a hero going home.

Tecumseh

The death of Billy Caldwell on September 28, 1841 was the beginning of the end of the Potawatomi tribe residency in Iowa. Caldwell died of cholera and was buried in the cemetery behind the blockhouse mission. When the blockhouse was demolished and the bluff lowered in 1857, the graves were moved to the "old Catholic cemetery." The St. Joseph Cemetery is believed to be the only "old Catholic cemetery" in present-day Council Bluffs.

Babbitt's research stated Caldwell appointed Joseph Robidoux to act at power of attorney while he was on buffalo hunts in order to protect his money. In June 1841, Caldwell attended a hunt in Sioux country. Caldwell returned from the hunting trip sick, and by August 22, 1841, he was seriously ill and unable to conduct business.

Clifton states following Caldwell's death, the Iowa Potawatomi petitioned the Commissioner of Indian Affairs to rename and be identified as "Prairie Indians of Caldwell's Band of the Pottawattomies." Clifton states Caldwell's name carried with it highly respected, supernormal power.

Following Caldwell's death, a treaty was signed on June 5, 1846 to move all Native Americans from Iowa to Kansas. Sometime after Caldwell's death and before the 1846 treaty was signed, it was recorded that Caldwell's wife died. As the time approached on October 11, 1846 the final removal of the Sacs and Foxes commenced. Col. Peter A. Sarpy oversaw the Potawatomi, Chippewa, and Ottawa Agency at Trader's Point on the Missouri river. Sarpy held a council with their representatives on June 5 and 17, 1845, and secured a treaty by which these tribes surrendered all claim to tracts north of the Missouri river and embraced in the limits of the Territory of Iowa.

Picture of an Iron Cross leaning against an old oak tree in the St. Joseph Cemetery where the Billy Caldwell Historical Marker is located. It is an anonymous iron marker signifying the quiet, gentleness of the rolling hills and mature oak trees in the old cemetery. (*Image courtesy of Susan L. Kelsey*)

The Caldwell band moved to Kansas and combined with members of the Mission Band (from Michigan), and over the course of the next fifteen years, this group eventually split into two diverse groups, the Citizen Potawatomi Nation and the Prairie Band Potawatomi Nation. The difference between the two groups was based on principal and theology about United States citizenship and federal allotments. Historically, the traditional Prairie Band declined citizenship and allotments. Citizen Potawatomi tribe agreed to citizenship and 160-acre allotments. The tribes divided their reservation in a treaty signed 1861.

Citizen Potawatomi Nation, Shawnee, Oklahoma

The Citizen Potawatomi Nation, Algonquin people with origins from the Great Lakes and the original Mission Band from Michigan, moved south from Kansas to Oklahoma in the early 1800s. In 1867, the tribe moved to Oklahoma, and in 1870–71, Citizen Potawatomi Nation moved to the area of Shawnee, Oklahoma. In 1889, the Nation lost most of their land but today is a federally recognized tribe with a Cultural Heritage Center, an Eagle Aviary, numerous enterprises, and more than 30,000 tribal citizens.

The Indian Census Rolls, 1885–1940 (M595, 692 rolls), were submitted each year by agents or superintendents in charge of Indian reservations to the Commissioner of Indian Affairs, as required by an act of July 4, 1884 (23 Stat. 98). The data on the rolls

Today's Citizen Band Potawatomi Nation located in Shawnee, Oklahoma, home to genealogy research, wonderful museum, and tribal business activities. (*Image courtesy of Susan L. Kelsey*)

vary, but usually given are the English and/or Indian name of the person, roll number, age or date of birth, sex, and relationship to head of family. Beginning in 1930, the rolls also include the degree of Indian blood, marital status, ward status, place of residence, and sometimes other information. For certain years—1935, 1936, 1938, and 1939—only supplemental rolls of additions and deletions were compiled. There is not a census for every reservation or group of American Indians for every year. Only persons who maintained a formal affiliation with a tribe under federal supervision are listed on these census rolls. These roles provided insight into which families travelled with Caldwell, which families remained with the Prairie Band, and which families left with the Citizen Band.

The Tribal Roles also assisted with research on family names (LaFramboise, Wilmet, Bertrand, Chevalier, Beaubien, Bourbonnais, Leclere, Bourassa, and Bertrand) that travelled with Caldwell throughout his life and carried his legacy to today.

Family genealogies recorded in present-day research include Catherine Welch's family. Catherine's family moved with Caldwell (Chief Sauganash) and the Chicago Potawatomi to the West. They first settled along the Missouri River, in what is now Buchanan County, Missouri, but could stay only a short time before a part of the tribe was moved on to the Council Bluffs, Iowa Reserve. Catherine's grandmother, Archange Wilmette (Ouilmette), died on the Reserve at Council Bluffs, in November 1840. Her grandfather, Antoine, passed away at the same place in December 1841. LaFramboise family moved to the Potawatomi Reservation and descendants are still present today.

The Prairie Band Potawatomi Nation, Silver Lake, Kansas

The Prairie Band Potawatomi Nation resides in Mayette, Kansas today. According to their website, the band originated from the Great Lakes and a small group of 780 members formed the Prairie Band Potawatomi Nation. The band was historically different than Citizen Band in that it believed in communal holdings. Decisions were made as a group and not individually. The website states, "they were neither interested in obtaining citizenship nor rejecting their heritage, and they held firm in their belief that no single person owned the land."

Prairie Band Chief Wabwabashkot resisted allotment until 1895 and tribal organization disintegrated afterwards. The Prairie Band Tribal Council ceased after 1900 and the agency closed in 1903 with annuities stopping six years later. The original Prairie Band reservation was over 11 square miles, located on the Kaw River and today only 22 percent remains in a scattered region. They are federally recognized today.

The Caldwell Band remained in Kansas with the Prairie Band. In Kansas, the Jesuit (Missouri Province, St. Louis) missions to the Potawatomi began in 1839. They opened a school for boys in 1840, and the following year, the Sisters of the Society of the Sacred Heart (St. Louis) opened a school for girls. Both schools closed in 1848 and were followed by St. Mary's Mission and school, which opened later that year at St. Mary's, Kansas, with staff from these religious orders. By the 1870s and to *c.* 1900, St. Mary's no longer served significant numbers of Potawatomi except through its station at Silver Lake.

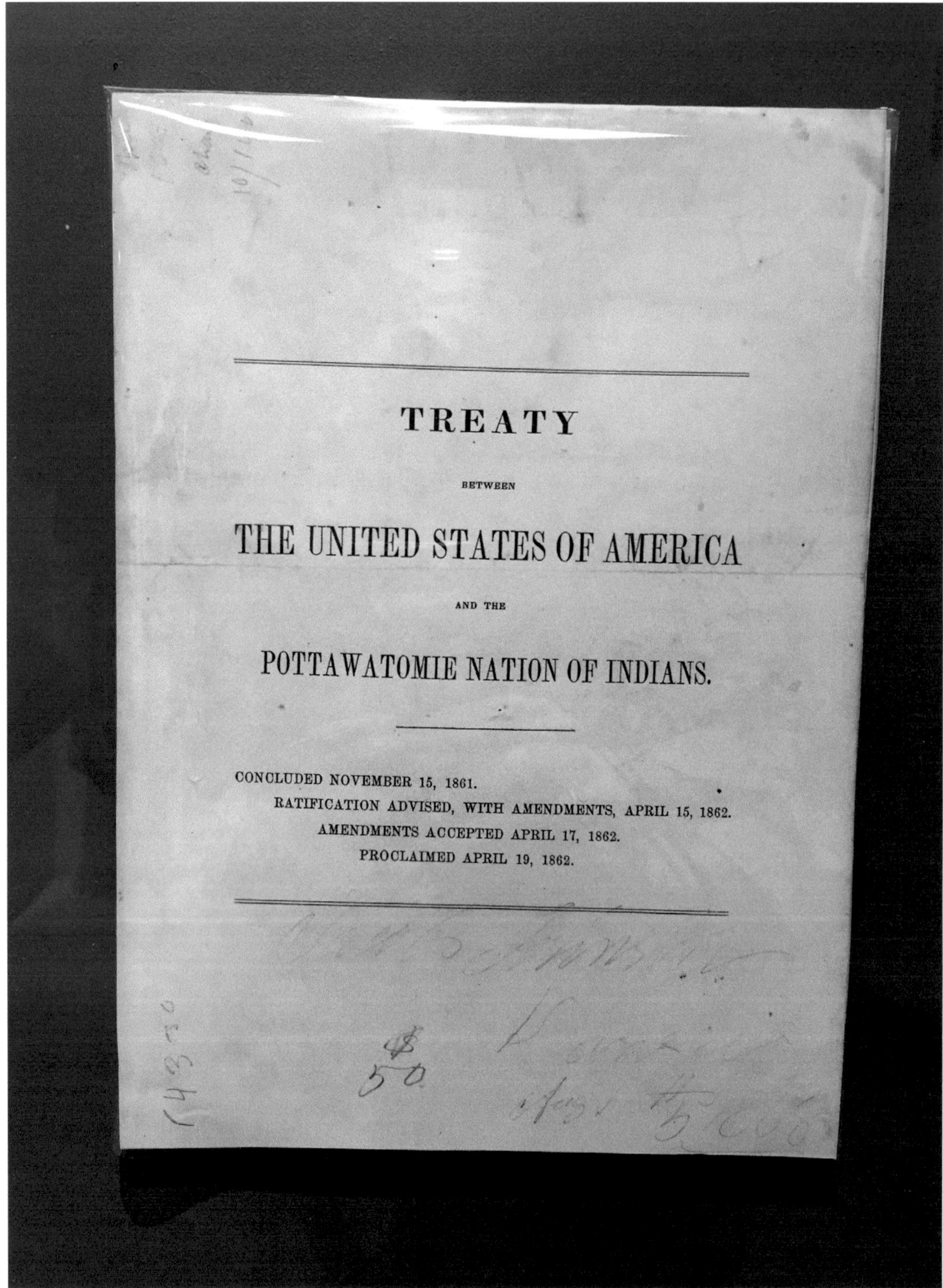
TREATY

BETWEEN

THE UNITED STATES OF AMERICA

AND THE

POTTAWATOMIE NATION OF INDIANS.

CONCLUDED NOVEMBER 15, 1861.
RATIFICATION ADVISED, WITH AMENDMENTS, APRIL 15, 1862.
AMENDMENTS ACCEPTED APRIL 17, 1862.
PROCLAIMED APRIL 19, 1862.

Indian Land Certificate located at the Citizen Band Potawatomi Museum. (*Image courtesy of Citizen Band Potawatomi Museum, photo by Susan L. Kelsey*)

Family genealogy collection at the Citizen Band Potawatomi Museum. (*Courtesy of the Citizen Band Potawatomi Museum, photo by Susan L. Kelsey*)

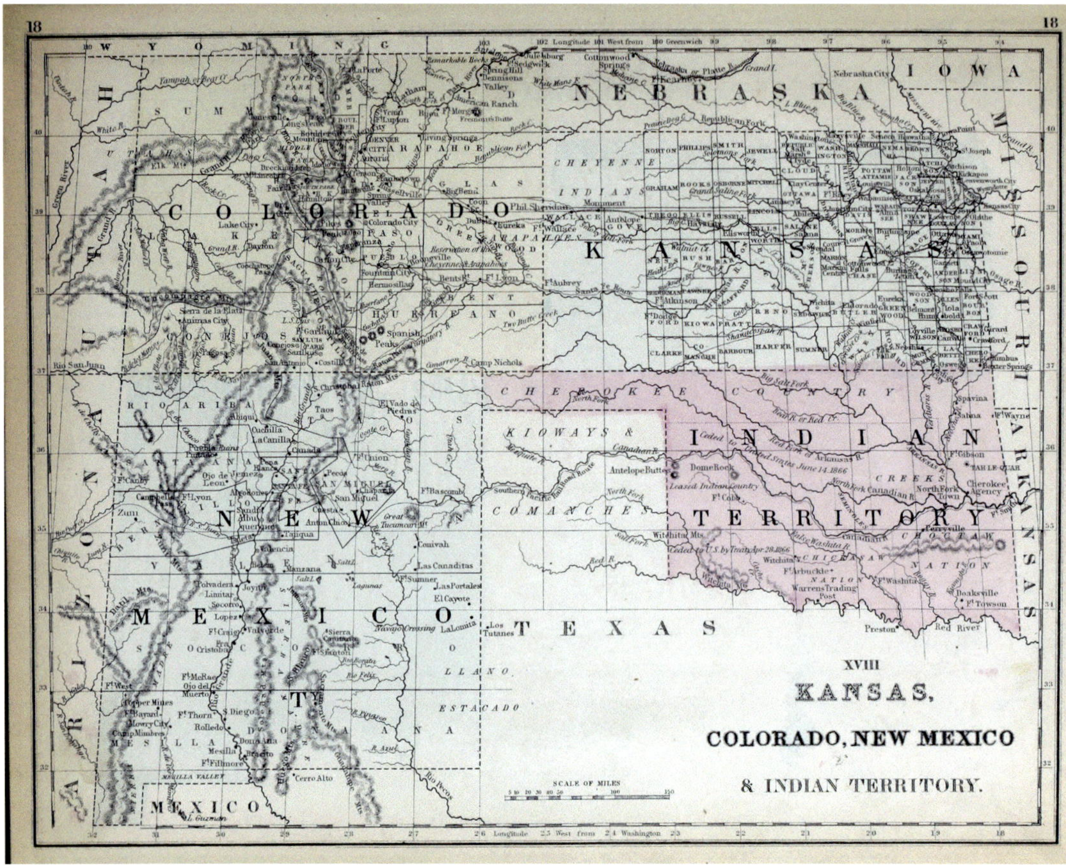

18
18
W Y O M I N G
NEBRASKA
IOWA
MISSOURI
COLORADO
KANSAS
CHEYENNE
INDIANS
CHEROKEE COUNTRY
INDIAN
TERRITORY
ARKANSAS
NEW
MEXICO.
TEXAS
LLANO
ESTACADO
UTAH
ARIZONA
MEXICO
XVIII
KANSAS,
COLORADO, NEW MEXICO
& INDIAN TERRITORY.
SCALE OF MILES

The Prairie Band Potawatomi Nation moved from Council Bluffs, Iowa, to a Kansas reservation. See map inset Pottawattomi County, Kansas. (*Image courtesy Susan L. Kelsey collection*)

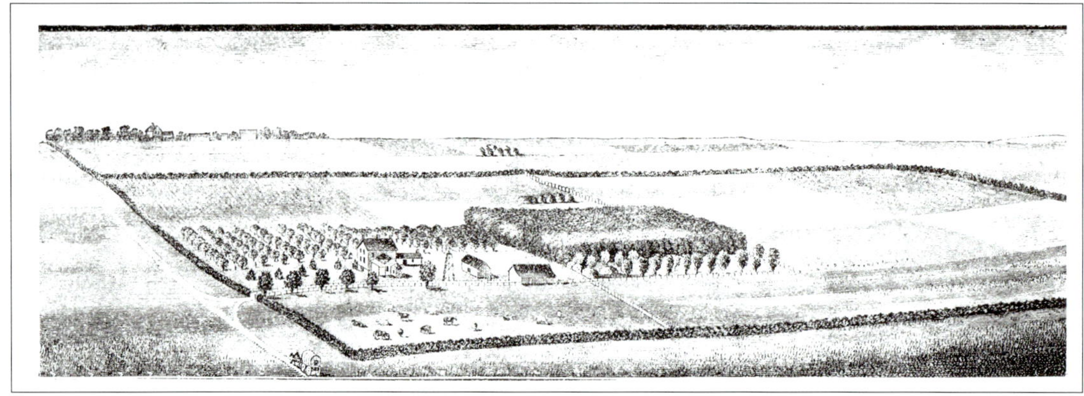

Kansas prairie farming mid-1800s. The Prairie Band Potawatomi Nation were entrepreneurs and capitalized on the rich prairie soil. (*Image from the collection of Susan L. Kelsey*)

These members were entrepreneurial in 1850s with the beginning of the gold rush. As people left the Kansas City area, after about 100 miles, they passed through the Prairie Band Potawatomi Nation for supplies and stopped in these communities.

The Prairie Band Potawatomi Nation website states: Two treaties, one in 1861 and another in 1867, carved the existing reservation with a land base of 568,223 acres into portions that accommodated individual interests. The railroad received over 338,000 acres, Jesuit interests 320 acres, Baptist interests 320 acres, and the rest was divided into separate plots. The Jesuits, although failing ultimately to make Kansas a center of Catholic interest, did eventually settle approximately 2,300 acres around St. Mary's Mission. With the conclusion of the railroad treaties of the 1860s, the Potawatomi settled upon the 11 square-mile reservation expecting to live in peace. But, as so many times in the past, continued development overlooked the interests of the tribe.

Today, according to the Prairie Band Potawatomi Nation website, based on an extensive administrative record, the Solicitor of the U.S. Department of the Interior issued a Solicitor's Opinion in 2001, concluding that: (1) the Shab-eh-nay (Chief Shabonna at Shabbona's Grove) reservation still exists; (2) the Nation is the legal successor-in-interest to the Shab-eh-nay Band; and (3) the United States continues to bear a trust responsibility to the Nation for these lands. In 2006, the Interior Department confirmed the 2001 Solicitor's Opinion.

The Billy Caldwell—Chief Sauganash Legacy

Chief Sauganash, a Native American also known as Billy Caldwell, played a critical role in early American and Chicago history. At an early age, Billy Caldwell struggled with identity, crossing the lines of British, Native America, and white, finally emerging as one of the leaders of the surrounding Native American communities. Such was the collective population of early Chicago; groups of Europeans, Native Americans, and people of mixed race who tried to blend in with both worlds.

Caldwell negotiated treaties with the United States on behalf of the United Nations of Potawatomi, Chippewa, and Ottawa and was one of the leading negotiators of the Chicago Treaty of 1833 and the relocation of the Potawatomi to southwest Iowa in 1837. He successfully negotiated over 5 million acres of land for the new America.

He spent his life working to gain the long-promised boundary by the British between the Indians and white settlers. In the end, he died with his tribe as an Indian on the banks of the Missouri River in Iowa. His body returned to the land on a Loess Hill in Council Bluffs, Iowa. Caldwell will always be remembered as an instrumental pioneer in the forming of a new city called Chicago, on the banks of Lake Michigan, on one of the five Great Lakes in America.

Epilogue

For over 170 years, researchers have been intrigued with the history of Billy Caldwell. To date, there are no known descendants of Billy Caldwell; however, on August 22, 2016, the author received a phone call from a person living in Kansas claiming to be a descendant of Billy Caldwell. Several family meetings have been held, D.N.A. testing completed, and work continues piecing together family history and legacy timelines.

On Monday, May 11, 2015, at 12 p.m., a ceremony was held at St. Joseph Cemetery in Council Bluffs, Iowa, to commemorate the role of Billy Caldwell and the Potawatomi Indians in Council Bluffs history. A historical marker, etched with a brief history of the story, was placed on the hillside of the bluff that is believed to be the burial site of Caldwell and the Potawatomi when the graves were moved from behind the St. Joseph Indian Mission in 1857.

The ceremony consisted of a welcome by master of ceremonies Fr. Paul Monahan (retired diocesan priest); a smudging, using white sage from the Six Nations Reserve in Ontario, Canada (Caldwell's birthplace) led by David Smith S. J. (former teacher of the Lakota at the Holy Rosary Mission in Pine Ridge, South Dakota), assisted by high school student, Joe Sneller (Cherokee Ancestry) and Owen Webster (Indian Center of Omaha); a brief history by Susan Kelsey; and remarks by Fr. Monahan and Mary Lou McGinn. Music was provided by Todd Waltemath of the Can Ku Luta Drum Group, Omaha, and Michael Murphy on Native American flute. The closing song was "America, the Beautiful."

A final offering of Native American tobacco was left beside the marker. A reception was held at the nearby Walnut Hill Reception Center.

A Kickstarter campaign launched by Susan Kelsey of Lake Forest, Illinois, raised $3,700 for the historical marker in celebration of Billy Caldwell's 235th birthday on March 17, 2015. The campaign was supported by the City of Council Bluffs, Iowa, and Preserve Council Bluffs.

CHIEF BILLY CALDWELL

Picture of Former Head of Pottawattamie Indians Is Desired for History.

If a daguerreotype or picture of Billy Caldwell, a former chief of the Pottawattamie Indians who settled on a reservation near this city in 18[illegible], is treasured among the archives of anyone in this section of the country, the author of a history of the Black Hawk war, which is in the course of preparation, would be pleased to have the privilege of using the picture to illustrate his book. The picture or information concerning it should be forwarded to Frank E. Stevens, 1206 Chamber of Commerce building, Chicago.

Concerning Chief Caldwell and the desire to secure a picture of him, Mr. Stevens says in a letter to The Nonpareil:

"In 18[illegible], when the Pottowattomie Indians were removed from Chicago and northern Illinois and Michigan to their new reservation near Council Bluffs, Billy Caldwell, one of their chiefs, went along and in the course of nature, died. Caldwell had been a man of great power and influence with his tribe and in the Black Hawk war was, with Shabbona, instrumental in dissuading his nation from joining the Sacs in their Illinois raid. For the use of a history of that Black Hawk war, I am very anxious to ascertain if Caldwell during his lifetime had ever a portrait made of himself. As daguerrotypes came into use in the early 40s it is possible he may have sat for one of that kind of pictures. At any rate, if there is a picture of him in existence I am very anxious to secure a copy of it.

"It has been suggested that I write a letter to The Nonpareil, asking if it would call the attention of its readers to my wants, and that if there existed a picture in the state of Iowa it could be thus located. May I therefore ask if you will kindly insert such an inquiry? While I am writing this letter from a personal standpoint, I am but voicing the desire of a number of people here who are very much interested in Indian history. I assure you the favor will be appreciated highly by all of us. Faithfully yours,

"FRANK E. STEVENS."

Jan 27, 1903

An article from 1903 from local author requesting photos of Chief Billy Caldwell. Even 100 years ago, people were interested in Caldwell, what he looked like and conducting research on his life and contributions to Pottawattomie County, Iowa. (*Image courtesy of the Nonpareil Newspaper, private collection of Mary Lou McGinn*)

Smudging at the Billy Caldwell Historical Marker dedication. The historical marker is located at the St. Joseph Cemetery, Council Bluffs, Iowa. (*Photo courtesy of Susan L. Kelsey*)

Above: Historical marker dedication ceremony. *From left to right*: Nonpareil newspaper photographer, musicians Todd Waltemath and Michael Murphy at St. Joseph Cemetery, Council Bluffs, Iowa. Billy Caldwell Historical Marker. (*Photo courtesy of Susan L. Kelsey*)

Below: The Billy Caldwell historical marker. The front of the marker states, "Billy Caldwell (Chief Sauganash). Born old Fort Niagara Canada March 17, 1780, died Council Bluffs, Iowa September 25, 1841. Son of Mohawk woman and an Irish captain in the British Army—Played important role in early Chicago history—negotiated 1833 Treaty of Chicago and led Potawatomi to local area in 1837. Welcomed Jesuits to establish St. Joseph Mission 1838–1841. Died in 1841—buried behind the mission." Located at the St. Joseph Cemetery, Council Bluffs, Iowa. Billy Caldwell Historical Marker (*Image courtesy of Susan L. Kelsey*)

Above: The back of the historical marker features three feathers, courtesy of Esther Stutzman. The marker states, Graves of those buried behind the mission were moved to the old Catholic cemetery in 1857. This site dedicated May 11, 2015. Two plaques at the east Pierce & Union mark the site of the St. Joseph Mission and old blockhouse. Located at Joseph Cemetery, Council Bluffs, Iowa. Billy Caldwell Historical Marker. (*Image courtesy of Susan L. Kelsey*)

Below: Mary Lou McGinn of Council Bluffs, Iowa, and Susan Kelsey of Lake Forest, Illinois, met through Mayor Matt Walsh and together raised over $3,700 for the Caldwell historical marker. Mary Lou, a lifelong resident of Council Bluffs, Iowa, has authored several historical books about Council Bluff homes. The St. Joseph Cemetery is located in Council Bluffs, Iowa, and the Billy Caldwell Historical Marker GPS Coordinates are: Latitude: 41.272576, Longitude: -95.822831. Caldwell is remembered often with gifts of tobacco, feathers, Irish flags, and other items left at the historical marker. (*Photo courtesy of Susan L. Kelsey*)

Acknowledgements

Thank you to Mary Lou McGinn of Council Bluffs, Iowa, for her passion in documenting accurate details of the life and times of Billy Caldwell; William Whittaker and his published work of mapping Caldwell's camp in Council Bluffs, Iowa; United States Library of Congress, National Archives of the United States, The Smithsonian National Museum of the American Indian, Crazy Horse Memorial and the National Indian Museum of North America, Musacchio family, Bobbi Roe, Elisabeth Cunnison, Mary Sanders, Dennis Downes and his lifetime work with the Great Lakes Trail Marker Tree Society; Dan Melone and his lifetime achievement of finding the Alexander Robinson family gravestones and burial grounds; Lawrence Pavia and Judy Heyworth of the Edgebrook-Sauganash Historical Society; Chicago Newberry Library; Chicago History Museum; the American Indian Center of Chicago; Mitchell Museum of the American Indian; Illinois State Historical Society, Lake County Illinois Historical Society; Wisconsin Historical Society; Department of Geology, Environmental and Spatial Sciences at Michigan State University; Prairie Research Institute at the University of Illinois Urbana-Champaign; Hauberg Blackhawk Indian Museum, St. Joseph Area Historical Society, Pony Express Museum, Agency Ford Museum, The State Historical Society of Missouri, New York Historical Society, Six Nations of the Grand River; Marsh Genealogy Center, Fort Niagara; Detroit Public Library, Detroit Historical Society, State Historical Society of Iowa; Office of the Mayor, Council Bluffs, Iowa; the Council Bluffs Daily Nonpareil Newspaper, Preserve Council Bluffs; Western Historic Trails Center; Council Bluffs Public Library; Prairie Band Potawatomi Nation; Citizen Band Potawatomi Nation; Canadian Museum of History; Anne Durkin Keating, *Rising up from Indian Country*; Marvin Recker (Caldwell timeline); the work of James A. Clifton; R. David Edmunds; and the work of Helen Hornbeck Tanner, the *Atlas of the Great Lakes Indian History*.

Bibliography

Alexander, L., *Sauganash: A Historical Perspective* (United States of America: 1999)

Andreas, A., *History of Cook County, Illinois, From the Earliest Period to the Present Time* (A.T.Andreas, Publisher, 1884)

Babbitt, C., *Early Days at Council Bluffs* (Washington, D.C., 1916); *The Old Pottawattamie Mill,* (The Palimpsest, 1925)

Baskin, O., *History of Pottawattomie County* (Iowa O.L. Baskin & Co. Historical Publishers, 1883)

Battin, W., and Frank, A., *Past and Present of Marshall County, Iowa* (United States of America: Brookhaven Press, 1912)

Benn, C., *Native Memories from the War of 1812* (Johns Hopkins University Press, 2014)

Bowes, J., *Exiles and Pioneers, Eastern Indians in the Trans-Mississippi West* (Cambridge University Press, 2007); *Land Too Good for Indians: Northern Indian Removal* (University of Oklahoma Press, 2016)

Brown, W., and Chicago Historical Society, *An historical sketch of the early movement in Illinois for the legalization of slavery, read at the annual meeting of the Chicago Historical Society, December 5th, 1864* (Goodman and Donnelley Chicago, 1865)

Butler, R., *Dictionary Catalog of the Edward E. Ayer Collection of Americana and American Indians in the Newberry Library* (United States of America: G. K. Hall, 1961)

Clarke, J., *Land, Power, and Economics on the Frontier of the Upper Canada* (United Kingdom: McGill-Queen's University Press, 2001)

Clifton, J., *The Prairie People: Continuity and Change in Potawatomi Indian Culture 1665–1965* (The Annals of Iowa 45 (1980), 237-239); *Merchant, soldier, broker, chief; a corrected obituary of Billy Caldwell* (Il State History Society Journey, 71 (1978): 185–210); *Billy Caldwell's exile in early Chicago*, (Chicago Historical Society, 1977); *The Pokagon's, 1683–1983*: *Catholic Potawatomi of the St. Joseph River Valley* (University Press of America, 1984)

Colbert, E. *Chicago and the Great Conflagration* (Applewood Books, 2009)

Colbert, E., and Chamberlin, E., *Chicago and the Great Conflagration* (C. F. Vent, 1871)

Currey, J. *Chicago: Its History and Its Builders: A Century of Marvelous Growth* (United States of America: S. J. Clarke Publishing Company, 1912)

Danckers, U., and Meredith, J., *Early Chicago* (Early Chicago Inc., 2000)

DeSmet, P., *Life, Letters and Travels of Father Pierre-Jean de Smet, S.J. 1801–1873; missionary labors and adventures among the wild tribes of the North American Indians* (New York, F.P. Harper, 1905)

East, E., *The Inhabitants of Chicago, 1825–1831* (Journal of Illinois State Historical Society, Vol. 37:2, June 1944)

Edmonds, R., *A history of the Potawatomi Indians*, (University of Oklahoma, 1972); *Kinsmen Through Time, An annotated Bibliography of Potawatomi History.* (The Scarecrow Press, Inc., Metuchen, N. J., 1987); *The Potawatomis: Keepers of the Fire.* (United Kingdom: University of Oklahoma Press, 1987)

Ellis, E. *The Indian Wars of the United States: From the First Settlement at Jamestown, in 1607, to the Close of the Great Uprising of 1890–91* (United States of America: Fb&c Limited, 2016. Fergus' Historical Series. United States of America: Fergus printing Company, 1884)

Fergus, Fergus' historical series (Chicago: Fergus Print. Co., 1876)

Garraghan, G., *The Catholic Church in Chicago, 1673–1871, An Historical Sketch* (Loyola University Press, 1921)

Goodspeed, W., and Healy, D., *History of Cook County*, Volume 1 (The Goodspeed Historical Association, 1909)

Grady, W. *The Great Lakes: The Natural History of a Changing Region* (Vancouver: Greystone Books, 2007)

Greusel, J., *Collections and researches made the Michigan Pioneer and Historical Society* (1910)

Gross, L., and Fay, H., *Past and Present of DeKalb County, Illinois* (United States of America: Pioneer Publishing Company, 1907)

Gue, B., *History of Iowa from the Earliest Times to the Beginning of the Twentieth Century* (Century History Company, 1903)

Haeger, J., *The American Fur Company and the Chicago of 1812–1835* (Journal of the Illinois State Historical Society 61 (1968): 117–139)

Haines, E., *The American Indian (Uh-nish-in-na-ba), The Whole Subject Complete in One Volume : Illustrated with Numerous Appropriate Engravings* (Chicago : Mas-sin-na'-gan Co., 1888)

Harper, J., *Guide to the Draper Manuscripts* (United States of America: Wisconsin Historical Society Press, 2014)

Illinois Catholic Historical Review (United States of America: Illinois Catholic Historical Society, 1922)

Illinois Catholic Historical Review, Volume 1, Number 2 (Illinois Catholic Historical Society, 1918)

James, C., *Early History of the Town of Amherstburg, A Short, Concise and Interesting Sketch with Explanatory Notes* (Echo Printing, 1902)

Journal of the Illinois State Historical Society, Volumes 55–56

Keating, A., *Rising Up from Indian Country: The Battle of Fort Dearborn and the Birth of Chicago* (University of Chicago Press, 2012)

Keating, W., *Narrative of an Expedition to the Source of St. Peter's River* (United States of America: University Press of the Pacific, 2003)

Kelly, R., *Chicago Big-Shouldered City* (Reilly & Lee Co., 1962)

Kelsey, S., *Following Chief Sauganash Captain Billy Caldwell (1780–1841)* (Iron Gate Production, Inc., 2016)

Kinzie, Mrs. John H.,*Wau-Bun, the Early Day of the North-West* (United States of America: D. B. Cooke, 1857)

Kirkland, J., *The Chicago Massacre of 1812* (Chicago Dibble Publishing Co., 1893)

Koester and Zander, *Sauganash, 1780–1848* (United States of America: Limited, 2018)

Landes, R., *Prairie Potawatomi: Tradition and Ritual in the Twentieth Center* (University of Wisconsin Press, 1970)

Lohmann, P., *Landforms of Iowa* (University of Iowa Press, Iowa City, 1991)

Malcomson, R., *Historical Dictionary of the War of 1812* (Scarecrow Press, 2006)

McDonald, D., *Removal of the Pottawattomi Indians from Northern Indiana* (Plymouth, Ind., D. McDonald & Co., 1899); *Removal of the Pottawattomie Indians from Northern Indiana; Embracing Also a Brief Statement of the Indian Policy of the Government, and Other Historical Matter Relating to the Indian Question* (Hansebooks, 2017)

McKee, I., *The Trail of Death: Letters of Benjamin Marie Petit* (Classic Reprint) (United States of America: 1kg Limited, 2017); *The Trail of Death: Letters of Benjamin Marie Petit* (Indiana Historical Society, 1941)

Murphy, J., *Potawatomi Indians of the West: Origins of the Citizen Band* (Citizen Band Potawatomi Tribe, Shawnee, OK, 1988)

Papers in Illinois History and Transactions for the Year—Illinois State Historical Society

Patterson, J. and Quaife, M., *Life of Black Hawk, Ma-ka-tai-me-she-kia-kiak—Black Hawk* (Sauk chief), (R. R. Donnelley & Sons Company, 1916)

Peterson, J., *Wild Chicago: The Formation and Destruction of a Multiracial Community on the Midwestern Frontier, 1816–1837 In The Ethnic Frontier*, ed. Melvin G. Holli and Peter d'A. Jones (1977, 25–71).

Pierce, B., *A History of Chicago, Volume 1, The Beginning of a City 1673–1848* (University of Chicago Press, 2007)

Pinther, M., and Tanner, H., *Atlas of Great Lakes Indian History* (United States of America: University of Oklahoma Press, 1987)

Prior, J., *Landforms of Iowa* (United States of America: University of Iowa Press, 1991)

Pruitt, O. J., *Indian Stories* (United States of America: Pottawattamie County Historical Society, 1959)

Quaife, M., *Chicago and the Old Northwest, 1673–1835, A Study of the Evolution of the Northwestern Frontier, Together with a History of Fort Dearborn* (University of Chicago Press, 1913)

Quimby, G., *Indian Life in the Upper Great Lakes* (The University of Chicago Press. 1960)

Rothensteiner, J., and Souvay, C., *Saint Louis Catholic Historical Review*, Volumes 2–3 (Catholic Historical Society of Saint Louis, 1923)

Ruth, L., *Prairie Potawatomi: Tradition and Ritual in the Twentieth Century* (University of Wisconsin Press, 1970)

Severance, F., *Old Trails on the Niagara Frontier* (United States of America: Matthews-Northup Company, 1899)

Stevens, W., *Centennial History of Missouri (the Center State) One Hundred Years in the Union, 1820–1921* (S. J. Clarke publishing company, 1921)

Tanner, H., *Atlas of Great Lakes Indian History* (University of Oklahoma Press, 1987)

Temple, W., *Shabbona: Friend of the Whites* (Springfield Illinois State Museum, 1957)

The Past & Present of La Salle County, Illinois: Containing a History of the County—its Cities, Towns, &c., a Biographical Directory of Its Citizens, War Record of Its Volunteers in the Late Rebellion, Portraits of Early Settlers & Prominent Men, General and Local Statistics, Map of La Salle County, History of Illinois, Constitution of the United States, Miscellaneous Matters, Etc. (United States of America: H. F. Kett & Company, 1877)

Valencius, C., *The Lost History of the New Madrid Earthquake* (The University of Chicago Press, 2013)

Weaks, M., Draper, L. C., *The Preston and Virginia Papers of the Draper Collection of Manuscripts* (United States of America: The Society, 1915)

Wentworth, J., *Early Chicago. Fort Dearborn, An Address Delivered at the Unveiling of the Memorial Tablet* (Hansebooks, 1917); *Reminiscences of Early Chicago* (R.R. Donnelley & Sons Company, 1912)

Willard, S., Campbell, S., and Petit, B., *Potawatomi Trail of Death: 1838 Removal from Indiana to Kansas* (Rochester, Ind: Fulton County Historical Society, 2003)

Winger, O., *The Potawatomi Indians* (The Elgin Press 1939)
Wishart, D., *The Fur Trade of the American West* (University of Nebraska Press, 1979)
Wm. Clark to John C. Calhoun, St. Louis, May 10, 1824 (Journal of Illinois State Historical Society, 1824)
Wood, N., *Lives of Famous Indian Chiefs, from Cofachiqui, the Indian Princess, and Powhatan; Down to and Including Chief Joseph and Geronimo* (American Indian historical publishing company, Aurora, Illinois, 1906)

Notes

The Draper Collections (Wisconsin State Historical Society, Madison). Lyman Draper biographic interviews with Mark Beaubien, Alexander Robinson, James and William Caldwell.

The Encyclopedia of Chicago. United Kingdom: University of Chicago Press, 2004.The history of the Pokagon Band of southwest Michigan, the Potawatomi's who were officially permitted to stay in their homeland

Timeline dates were collected from various sources. Some of these dates were confirmed from Marvin Recker timeline, descendent of Billy Caldwell's father, William Caldwell, Sr, Canada; Early Chicago, Danckers & Meredith, 1999 and bibliography resources.

Virgil J. Vogel Research and Personal Papers, The Newberry Library, and Chicago.

Index